THE ENGLISH NOVEL 1578-1956

A Checklist of Twentieth-Century Criticisms

THE ENGLISH NOVEL
1578 - 1956

A Checklist

of

Twentieth-Century Criticisms

INGLIS F. BELL
and
DONALD BAIRD

ALAN SWALLOW
Denver

Copyright 1958 by Inglis F. Bell and Donald Baird

Library of Congress Card Number: 59—8212

Ref
PR
821
.Z99
B4

PREFACE

The compilers of this checklist had long felt the need for easy access to published analyses of novels when they first came upon <u>Poetry Explication</u>. The usefulness of the Arms and Kuntz bibliography further convinced them that a similar checklist of analyses of novels would be worthwhile.

We began the project by limiting the search to twentieth century criticisms of English novels from John Lyly's <u>Euphues</u> to those of such contemporary novelists as Graham Greene. Approximately 2000 monographs and the files of over 100 periodicals were searched. The checklist is selective in that expositions of plot and eulogizing commentaries were excluded.

We wish to acknowledge with thanks the assistance of Ronald Baker, John Creighton, Elliott Gose, Stanley Read, and George Woodcock of the University of British Columbia English Department; Neal Harlow, Samuel Rothstein and George G. Turner of the University of British Columbia Library; Joan Selby of the Vancouver Public Library; Miss Anne Melanson of the University of British Columbia Extension Department; the Library of the University of California at Berkeley and especially to Rocco Crachi of that University; the University of Alberta for a grant to assist in the preparation of manuscript; and the University of British Columbia for a grant-in-aid of research.

CONTENTS

PREFACE

INTRODUCTION ii

CHECKLIST 1

SOURCES 143

INTRODUCTION

Many distinguished critics have said that criticism of the English novel did not exist in the nineteenth century and that there have been few close critical analyses in the twentieth. Henry James remarked in "The Art of Fiction" (1884) that the English novel " . . . had no air of having a theory, a conviction, a consciousness of itself behind it - - of being the expression of an artistic faith, the result of choice and comparison,"[1] and, that " . . . there was a comfortable good-humoured feeling abroad, that a novel is a novel, as a pudding is a pudding and that our only business with it could be to swallow it."[2] Over sixty years later (1952) Mark Schorer reiterated James's widely circulated opinion of nineteenth century criticism,[3] and about the same time (1951) Arnold Kettle commented on " . . . the lack of analysis and of disciplined critical evaluation . . ."[4] in the contemporary criticism of the novel.

These statements are valid to the extent that the second

stage in the criticism of the novel, marked by the publication of James's prefaces,* did not arrive until the first decade of the Twentieth century; that not until the third stage, in the mid-twentieth century, did close critical analysis of the novel begin; and that previous to James only first principles - - plot, character, and style - - had been advanced.

But it is important to note that they had been advanced and indeed long applied. These admittedly primary concepts have been recently in bad odor, not so much from any lack of validity as from misuse, just as the excesses of the third stage - - the analytical - - are now placing this critical technique in some disrepute. Yet the early concepts of character and plot do mean something, if only an awareness of consistency in characterization and of plot as a means of character motivation and development. When James or a mid-twentieth-century critic speaks of the complete lack of criticism of the English novel in the nineteenth century, he does so because little genuine use was made of the limited critical apparatus and vocabulary available, and because there was almost no awareness, in the consideration of character, plot, and style, of the inter-relationships of the parts and the oneness of the whole.

Admittedly, nineteenth and early twentieth-century criticism of the novel in terms of character, plot, and style did invite a non-literary scrutiny, resulting, often, in appreciations irrelevant to the novel as an art form. The term "character," for example, led to discussion of the novel's personae as individuals dissociated from context. As late as 1913 a major critic, Saintsbury, elaborates Lovelace as

> . . . handsome, haughty, arbitrary, as well as rich, generous after a fashion, well descended, well dressed, well mannared - - except when he is insolent. He is also - - which certainly stands to his credit in the bank which is not that of the snob

---

* To the New York Edition of the Novels and Tales published by Scribner 1907-1909.

or the schoolgirl - - no fool in a general way. But he is not in the least a gentleman except in externals; and there is really nothing "great" about him at all. Even his scoundrelism is mostly, if not wholly, pose - - which abominable thing indeed distinguishes him throughout, in every speech and every act, from the time when he sighs as he kisses Miss Arabella Harlow's hand to the time when he says, "Let this expiate!" as that hallowed sword of Colonel Morden's passes through his rotten heart.[5]

What he says is perhaps true, but is it worth saying except in the (one suspects critically unconscious) allusion to character consistency? He is not criticizing the character in relation to Richardson's novel; he is recreating it.

Plot, character, style, and background, in the first and in the early second stage of criticism, were thought of as seaparate entities. The characters were buoyant, witty, manly, delicate, or "powerful creations"; the plot well-knit or filled wity a variety of rich episodes; the style an attractive embellishment. David Masson could say in 1859," . . . in a novel, if the writer can contrive, consistently with poetic method, or even sometimes by a slight strain on that method, to give us valuable matter over and above the mere fiction or story, we ought to allow all that is given to go to his credit,"[6] and further, " . . . much of the interest depends on the author's power of description, i.e. on his faculty in the imagination of scenery . . . . "[7] It is apparent that little thought was given, in the nineteenth century, to consideration of the novel as an artistic whole. This should not obscure the fact that there was criticism if only at an elementary level. The most notable thing about this first stage and the early years of the second was not a total lack of criticism, but, before James, its tortoise-like advance, and, following James, the slow recognition and application of his critical theories.

The reason for the slow development of critical theory and practice in the nineteenth century can probably be found in the inferior status of the novel in relation to poetry. The novel did not receive the same critical attention as poetry because critics devoted their energies to what they considered the higher form of literature. Of those in the nineteenth century who considered the novel an art form at all, David Masson reflects the typical attitude:

> Hence in general though not universally high, serious, and very heroic themes of poetic interest beg, and almost claim, by right of fitness or precedent, to be invested with the garb of verse; leaving to prose such as are of plainer or rougher, or less sublime and impassioned character.[8]

It is apparent that the novel was undergoing in the nineteenth century the same struggle for artistic recognition that the English drama underwent in the sixteenth. Moreover, this struggle for status, it is evident, is only now being won. In 1941 Lionel Trilling wrote that the novel is "the least artistic of the genres."[9] On the other side, Allen Tate in 1944[10] and Mark Schorer in 1949[11] felt it necessary to make the assertion that "fiction is an art."

An indication of the novel's inferior reputation, almost from the beginning, can be seen in the many attempts to call it by another name. Fielding referred to his stories as "histories" or "comic epics in prose" and later, after the great flood of cheap "circulating library" and "yellow back" fiction had further reduced the status of the novel, it became quite common to differentiate between the novel and the romance. In the twentieth century we see an indication of this qualitative differentiation in Graham Greene's distinction between "novels" and "entertainments." When novels were not called out-and-out by another name, attempts were made to justify their existence by attaching to them some useful purpose, most often the imparting of knowledge, historical, social, or moral. Attributing a moral function to the novel was, no doubt, a defence against the widely prevailing feeling that the novel, together with the stage, drinking, gambling, and card-playing, was immoral.

Probably the most serious obstacle to the recognition of the novel as an art form - - the equal of poetry - - has been the attitude of the academician, described by Henry Canby in 1922 as the " ... Brahman among American readers of fiction . . . the college professor of English . . . " and he continues:

> . . . in all this the college professor is profoundly justified by tradition . . . To him belongs that custody of the classical in literature which his profession inherited from the monasteries, and more remotely from the rhetoricians of Rome .... Our college professors . . . still doubt the artistic validity in a form never dignified by the practice of the ancients, like much of English literature besides, by a long line of native productions adapting classic forms to new ages and new speech.[12]

The English novel had some difficulty breaking through this barricade of academic hostility into the college calendar. William Lyon Phelps in his Autobiography[13] and Wilbur L. Cross in Connecticut Yankee[14] recount the difficulties they had in introducing courses on the English novel into the Yale curriculum. In 1895/96, Professor Phelps gave the first course in any university on the contemporary novel but was forced to drop it after one year because of the disapproval of the senior professors. There was, incidentally, a great deal of newspaper publicity given throughout the United States and England to this revolutionary innovation to the college curriculum. Professor Cross announced a graduate course in the English novel for the academic year 1896/97 but like Professor Phelps was asked to withdraw it. The opposition to the introduction of these two courses into the college curriculum typifies the university attitude towards the novel at the end of the nineteenth century.

With the prefaces, essays and novels of Henry James, an experimental period in the writing and criticism of the English novel began. Before James, English and American novelists were as little conscious of the possibilities of form as critics were of anything beyond first principles. James's abiding interest, on the other hand, was in technique. "One's work," he said, "should have composition, because composition alone is positive beauty."[15] In long prefaces

James analyzed the composition and the compositional successes and failures of his novels. His aim, the prefaces show, was to render his story dramatically and impersonally by the choice of a compositional centre; " . . . and to wave away the seated mass of explanation after the fact, the inserted block of merely referential narrative"[16] by the shifting of focus and the use of ficelles. He was the first English critic and novelist consciously and painstakingly to investigate, theorize, and elaborate on point of view, described by Allen Tate as "perhaps the distinctive feature of the modern novel."[17] James's remarks were not the first on point of view but they served to crystallize the theory and became the source of twentieth-century criticism of the novel. Since James's pioneer theorizing, this landmark of critical theory has been widely commented on. Joseph Warren Beach, in The Twentieth Century Novel, asserts, "In a bird's-eye-view of the English novel from Fielding to Ford, the one thing that will impress you more than any other is the disappearance of the author"[18]; Allen Tate, in "The Post of Observation in Fiction," says, "The limited and thus credible authority for the action, which is gained by putting the knower of the action inside its frame, is perhaps the distinctive feature of the modern novel . . ."[19]; and Percy Lubbock, in The Craft of Fiction, comments that "The Art of fiction does not begin until the novelist thinks of his story as a matter to be shown. . . ."[20] Notable studies on point of view began appearing shortly after James's death. The first of these, Joseph Warren Beach's The Method of Henry James,[21] was published in 1918. Between the study of Percy Lubbock, who systematized the theories of James in The Craft of Fiction[22] in 1921, and Norman Friedman's "Point of View in Fiction: The Development of a Critical Concept"[23] in 1955, the problem of point of view has become an important and standard section in all critical studies of the novel.

The prefaces and novels of Henry James ushered in a period of vigorous experimentation in fiction techniques. Novelists were concerned mainly with two: symbolism, deriving, as Bradford Booth says, " . . . from the spreading conviction that the novel should have a tighter form, a more considered style, and above all, concentration"[24]; and stream of consciousness, which changed not only the form of the novel but also its subject. The new, symbolical, tightly structural form and subjective, sometimes lyrical, content brought the novel closer to poetry with a consequent advance in its status as an art form.

At the same time, the vast majority of critics were still concerned almost exclusively with the criticism of poetry. By the early 1930's a new and radical development in criticism had occurred. Explication - - the new criticism - - ushered in by I.A. Richards' Practical Criticism[25] in 1929 was applied at first almost solely to poetry; but within two decades its army of practitioners made a complete about-face and criticism of the novel had begun to catch up with that of poetry as John Aldridge points out in his preface to Critiques and Essays on Modern Fiction.[26]

There were three main reasons for the shift of criticism from poetry to fiction. During the experimental period the novel had been refined and developed to a point which gave critics extended possibilities for explication. Moreover the reader of the contemporary novels of James, Conrad, Joyce, Lawrence, and Woolf required the analytic assistance of the critic. Thirdly, because of the difficult and indeed baffling poetry of the Eliot metaphysical school even the learned reader was turning from poetry to fiction. The critic of course followed. "The movement was," as Alan Swallow remarks, "almost en masse to fiction. As a quick estimate, now it seems that nearly seven out of ten manuscripts being submitted are about fiction."[27] A check of this bibliography indicates the trend; of the 490 periodical entries, seventy-two percent have appeared in the last decade.

The university attitude too had undergone a change. The early histories of the novel by Tuckuman(1882), Lanier(1883), Crawford(1893), Raleigh(1894), Cross(1899), Saintsbury(1913), and Phelps (1916); the critical prefaces and essays of James; and the early experiments in technique by James, Conrad, Ford, and others brought to the novel a degree of academic respectability. Professor Schellor, in the vanguard, offered the first college level course in the United States on the English novel at the University of Pennsylvania in 1889/90. Chicago, Cornell, Western Reserve, and Wisconsin listed courses in 1892, Minnesota in 1894, and Yale in 1895. Professor Phelps' course at Yale in 1895 was the first university course on the the contemporary novel. In 1897, Professor Cross was allowed to give at Yale, the course in the history of the novel which he had been forced to withdraw in 1896. Since the 1890s the history of the novel has been slowly added year by year to the curriculum of American and Canadian universities, and by 1940 most universities offered this one course. The shift in the emphasis of literary criticism in the late 1940s resulted in a similar though less spectacular shift in the universities. Up to 1945 most universities had given only one course on the novel. By 1955 several universities were giving from four to eight. Explicaté criticism, a critical technique offering wide scope to teachers and students, is largely responsible for the addition of courses.

The novel is now a recognized art form. Criticism of the novel, as Aldridge states, " . . . has begun to catch up with that of poetry . . . [although] we have not yet formulated it, or codified its insights or dignified it with a term, as we certainly shall do, and as we have already done with the criticism of poetry."[28] It is obvious from a review of current literature that the unanimity necessary to bring this millennium about is not as imminent as Mr. Aldridge's statement would seem to indicate. There remains a wide area of dispute over critical method and nomenclature. The assumption of the "new critics," reflected in Mark Schorer's already famous claim that "When we speak of technique, then, we speak of nearly everything"[29], is sharply disputed by David Daiches.[30] Philip Rahv attacks[31] and Stallman as heatedly defends[32] the methods and techniques of the "new critics." Disagreement continues between the "academic critics" and the "practical critics." No consensus of of opinion exists permitting formulation of a generally acceptable critical vocabulary. The validity of the terms character, plot, and and style, long questioned by many of the "new critics," has recently received well argued support from Robert Liddell,[33] and from Douglas Grant,[34] who concludes that these terms should not be jettisoned, but should be re-examined and revalued.

This present interest of critics in the novel, the effort to codify critical methods, and the search for a generally acceptable critical vocabulary will, the compilers hope, justify this bibliography. We also hope, by making a reasonably complete list of criticisms available, to indicate areas of research until now overlooked.

Inglis F. Bell
September, 1958

FOOTNOTES

1 Henry James. "The Art of Fiction," **Longman's Magazine** 4:502, September 1884. Reprinted in his **Partial Portraits**, London, Macmillan, 1911.

2 Henry James. "The Art of Fiction", as revised in his **Partial Portraits**, London, Macmillan, 1911. p. 376.

3 Mark Schorer. Foreword to John W. Aldridge, ed., **Critiques and Essays on Modern Fiction, 1920-1951**. New York, Ronald Press, 1952. p. xii.

4　Arnold Kettle. **An Introduction to the English Novel.** London, Hutchinson's University Library, 1951. Vol. 1. p. 7.

5　George Saintsbury. **The English Novel.** London, J.M. Dent, 1913. p. 96.

6　David Masson. **British Novelists and Their Styles.** Cambridge, Macmillan, 1859. p. 31.

7　**Ibid.** p. 27.

8　**Ibid.** p. 9.

9　Lionel Trilling. "Art and Fortune," In his **The Liberal Imagination.** New York, Viking Press, 1940. p. 278.

10　Allen Tate. "Techniques of Fiction," **Sewanee Review** 52:219, Spring 1944.

11　Mark Schorer. "Fiction and the 'Analogical Matrix'," **Kenyon Review** 11:539, Autumn 1949.

12　Henry Seidel Canby. "A Certain Condescension Toward Fiction," In his **Definitions.** New York, Harcourt, Brace, 1922. p. 46-48.

13　William Lyon Phelps. **Autobiography with Letters.** New York, Oxford University Press, 1939. p. 297-302.

14　Wilbur L. Cross. **Connecticut Yankee, An Autobiography.** New York, Yale University Press, 1943. p. 116-118.

15　Henry James. **The Art of the Novel.** London, Charles Scribner's Sons, 1935. p. 319.

16　**Ibid.** p. 321.

17　Allen Tate. "The Post of Observation in Fiction," **Maryland Quarterly** No. 2 p. 63. March 1944.

18　Joseph Warren Beach. **The Twentieth Century Novel.** New York, The Century Co., 1932. p. 14.

19　Tate, **op. cit.**, p. 63.

20　Percy Lubbock. **The Craft of Fiction.** London, Cape, 1921. p. 62.

21　Joseph Warren Beach. **The Method of Henry James.** Yale University Press, 1918.

22 Lubbock, **op. cit.**

23 Norman Friedman. "Point of View in Fiction: The Development of a Critical Concept," **PMLA** 70:1160-1184, December 1955.

24 Bradford A. Booth. "The Novel," In Lewis Leary, ed. **Contemporary Literary Scholarship.** New York, Appleton-Century-Crofts, 1958. p.271.

25 I.A. Richards. **Practical Criticism.** London, Kegan Paul, Trench, Trubner, 1929.

26 John Aldridge. **Critiques and Essays on Modern Fiction, 1920-1951.** New York, Ronald Press, 1952.

27 Alan Swallow. Editorial, **Twentieth Century Literature,** July 1957.

28 Aldridge, **op. cit.**, p. iii-iv.

29 Mark Schorer. "Technique as Discovery," In John W. Aldridge, ed. **Critiques and Essays on Modern Fiction, 1920-1951.** New York, Ronald Press, 1952. p. 67. Reprinted from **Hudson Review,** Spring 1948.

30 David Daiches. "The 'New Criticism': Some Qualifications," In his **Literary Essays.** Edinburgh, Oliver and Boyd, 1956.

31 Philip Rahv. "Fiction and the Criticism of Fiction," **Kenyon Review** 18:276-299, Spring 1956.

32 Robert Stallman. "Fiction and Its Critics: A Reply to Mr. Rahv," **Kenyon Review** 19:290-299, Spring 1957.

33 Robert Liddell. **A Treatise on the Novel.** London, Jonathan Cape, 1947.

34 Douglas Grant. "The Novel and Its Critical Terms," **Essays in Criticism** 1:421-429, October 1951.

CHECKLIST

AUSTEN, JANE

EMMA

Bailey, John Cann. **Introductions to Jane Austen.** London, Oxford University Press, 1931. p. 65-77.

Duffy, Joseph M. "Emma: The Awakening from Innocence." **ELH** 21:39-53, March 1954.

Edgar, Pelham. **The Art of the Novel from 1700 to the Present Time.** New York, Macmillan, 1933. p. 94-101.

Firkins, Oscar W. **Jane Austen.** New York, Holt, 1920. p. 96-115.

Hayes, E.N. "**Emma:** A Dissenting Opinion." **Nineteenth-Century Fiction** 4:1-20, June 1949. Reply by William Frost 4:325-8, March 1950.

Kettle, Arnold. **An Introduction to the English Novel.** London, Hutchinson's, 1951-53. V. 1 p. 90-104

The English Novel

McCullough, Bruce Welker. **Representative English Novelists: Defoe to Conrad.** New York, Harper, 1946. p. 101-112.

Mudrick, Marvin. **Jane Austen.** Princeton, Princeton University Press, 1952. p. 181-206.

Murray, James Gregory. "Measure and Balance in Jane Austen's **Emma.**" **College English** 16:160-166, December 1954.

Shannon, Edgar F., Jr. "**Emma:** Character and Construction." **PMLA** 71:637-650, September 1956.

Wright, Andrew H. **Jane Austen's Novels.** London, Chatto, 1953. p. 134-160.

LADY SUSAN

Mudrick, Marvin. **Jane Austen.** Princeton, Princeton University Press, 1952. p. 127-140.

MANSFIELD PARK

Bailey, John Cann. **Introductions to Jane Austen.** London, Oxford University Press, 1931. p. 50-64.

Collins, Barbara Bail. "Jane Austen's Victorian Novel." **Nineteenth-Century Fiction** 4:175-185, December 1949.

Duffy, Joseph M. "Moral Integrity and Moral Anarchy in **Mansfield Park,**" **ELH** 23:71-91, March 1956.

Firkins, Oscar W. **Jane Austen.** New York, Holt, 1920. p. 65-95.

Leavis, Q.D. "A Critical Theory of Jane Austen's Writings (II): **Lady Susan** into **Mansfield Park.**" **Scrutiny** 10:114-42, 1941.

— — — — —. "A Critical Theory of Jane Austen's Writings (II): **Lady Susan** into **Mansfield Park** (ii)." **Scrutiny** 10:272-94, 1942.

Mudrick, Marvin. **Jane Austen.** Princeton, Princeton University

Twentieth Century Criticisms

    Press, 1952. p. 155-180.

    Scrutton, Mary. "Bourgeois Cinderellas." **Twentieth Century.** 155:360-363, April 1954.

    Trilling, Lionel. "**Mansfield Park.**" Partisan Review 21: 492-511, September 1954.

    — — — — —. The Opposing Self; Nine Essays in Criticism. New York, Viking Press, 1955. p. 206-230.

    Wright, Andrew H. **Jane Austen's Novels.** London, Chatto, 1953. p. 123-134.

NORTHANGER ABBEY

    Bailey, John Cann. **Introductions to Jane Austen.** London, Oxford University Press, 1931. p. 78-92.

    Firkins, Oscar W. **Jane Austen.** New York, Holt, 1920. p. 49-64.

    Mathison, John K. "**Northanger Abbey** and Jane Austen's Conception of the Value of Fiction." **ELH** 24:138-152, June, 1957.

    Mudrick, Marvin. **Jane Austen.** Princeton, Princeton University Press, 1952. p. 37-58.

    Sadleir, Michael. **Things Past.** London, Constable, 1944. p. 167-200.

    Wright, Andrew H. **Jane Austen's Novels.** London, Chatto, 1953. p. 95-105.

PERSUASION

    Bailey, John Cann. **Introductions to Jane Austen.** London, Oxford University Press, 1931. p. 93-111.

    Cohen, Louise D. "Insight, the Essence of Jane Austen's

Artistry." **Nineteenth-Century Fiction** 8:213-224, December 1953.

Duffy, Joseph M. "Structure and Idea in Jane Austen's **Persuasion.**" **Nineteenth-Century Fiction** 8:272-289, March 1954.

MacCarthy, Sir Desmond. **Criticism.** London, Putnam, 1932. p. 230-234.

Mudrick, Marvin. **Jane Austen.** Princeton, Princeton University Press, 1952. p. 207-240.

Schorer, Mark. "Fiction and the 'analogical matrix'." In John W. Aldridge. **Critiques and Essays on Modern Fiction, 1920-1951.** New York, Ronald Press, 1952. p. 83-86. Also in **Kenyon Review** 11:540-544, Autumn, 1949.

Wright, Andrew H. **Jane Austen's Novels.** London, Chatto, 1953. p. 160-172.

PRIDE AND PREJUDICE

Bailey, John Cann. **Introductions to Jane Austen.** London, Oxford University Press, 1931. p. 35-49.

Brower, Reuben A. "The Controlling Hand: Jane Austen and **Pride and Prejudice.**" **Scrutiny** 13:99-111, 1945.

— — — — —. **The Fields of Light.** New York, Oxford University Press, 1951. p. 164-181.

Bush, Douglas. "Mrs. Bennet and the Dark Gods: the Truth about Jane Austen." **Sewanee Review** 64:591-596, Autumn 1956.

Firkins, Oscar W. **Jane Austen.** New York, Holt, 1920. p.24-48.

Kliger, Samuel. "Jane Austen's **Pride and Prejudice** in the Eighteenth-Century Mode." **University of Toronto Quarterly** 16:357-370, July 1947.

Mudrick, Marvin. **Jane Austen.** Princeton, Princeton University

Twentieth Century Criticisms

    Press, 1952. p. 94-126.

    Priestley, John Boynton. **The English Comic Characters.** London, J. Lane, 1928. p. 158-177.

    Schorer, Mark. "Pride Unprejudiced." **Kenyon Review.** 18: 72-91, Winter, 1956.

    Van Ghent, Dorothy. **The English Novel.** New York, Rinehart, 1953. p. 99-111.

    Wright, Andrew H. **Jane Austen's Novels.** London, Chatto, 1953. p. 105-123.

SANDITION

    Mudrick, Marvin. **Jane Austen.** Princeton, Princeton University Press, 1952. p. 241-258.

SENSE AND SENSIBILITY

    Bailey, John Cann. **Introductions to Jane Austen.** London, Oxford University Press, 1931. p. 23-34.

    Firkins, Oscar W. **Jane Austen.** New York, Holt, 1920. p.3-23.

    Mudrick, Marvin. **Jane Austen.** Princeton, Princeton University Press, 1952. p. 60-93.

    Wright, Andrew H. **Jane Austen's Novels.** London, Chatto, 1953. p.85-95.

THE WATSONS

    Mudrick, Marvin. **Jane Austen.** Princeton, Princeton University Press, 1952. p. 140-154.

BEACONSFIELD, BENJAMIN DISRAELI

    ENDYMION

        Speare, Morris Edmund. **The Political Novel.** New York, Oxford University Press, 1924. p. 119-142.

SYBIL

>Speare, Morris Edmund. **The Political Novel.** New York, Oxford University Press, 1924. p. 71-80.

BECKFORD, WILLIAM

VATHEK

>Conant, Martha Pike. **The Oriental Tale in England in the Eighteenth Century.** New York, Columbia University Press, 1908 (Columbia University Studies in English and Comparative Literature No. 17) p. 61-71.

BEHN, APHRA

OROONOKO

>Sypher, Wylie, "A Note on the Realism of Mrs. Behn's **Oroonoko**" **Modern Language Quarterly** 3:401-5, September 1942.

BENNETT, ARNOLD

CLAYHANGER

>Allen, Walter Ernest. **Arnold Bennett.** Denver, A. Swallow, 1949. p. 76-82.

>Hackett, Francis. **Horizons; a Book of Criticism.** New York, Huebsch, 1919. p. 147-155.

>Lafourcade, Georges. **Arnold Bennett.** London, Muller, 1939. p. 121-147.

>Scott-James, Rolfe Arnold. **Personality in Literature,** 1913-1931. New York, Holt, 1932. p. 87-90.

HILDA LESSWAYS

Twentieth Century Criticisms

    Scott-James, Rolfe Arnold. **Personality in Literature, 1913-1931.** New York, Holt, 1932. p. 91-95.

THE OLD WIVES' TALE

    Allen, Walter Ernest. **Arnold Bennett.** Denver, A. Swallow, 1949. p. 61-74.

    Brewster, Dorothy. **Modern Fiction.** New York, Columbia University Press, 1934. p. 94-101.

    Hackett, Francis. **Horizons; a Book of Criticism.** New York, Huebsch, 1919. p. 139-146.

    Lafourcade, Georges. **Arnold Bennett.** London, Muller, 1939. p. 96-120.

    Kettle, Arnold. **An Introduction to the English Novel.** London, Hutchinson's, 1951-53. v.2 p. 85-89.

    McCullough, Bruce Welker. **Representative English Novelists: Defoe to Conrad.** New York, Harper, 1946. p. 310-319.

    Scott-James, Rolfe Arnold. **Personality in Literature, 1913-1931.** New York, Holt, 1932. p. 81-86.

    Simons, J.B. **Arnold Bennett and His Novels.** Oxford, B. Blackwell, 1936. p.99-151.

THE PRETTY LADY

    Lafourcade, Georges. **Arnold Bennett.** London, Muller, 1939. p. 175-184.

RICEYMAN STEPS

    Allen, Walter Ernest. **Arnold Bennett.** Denver A. Swallow, 1949. p. 90-98.

    Lafourcade, Georges. **Arnold Bennett.** London, Muller, 1939. p. 184-195.

THESE TWAIN

    Hackett, Francis. **Horizons; a Book of Criticism.** New York, Huebsch, 1919. p. 156-162.

BOWEN, ELIZABETH

  THE DEATH OF THE HEART

    Strong, Leonard Alfred George. **Personal Remarks.** London, P. Nevill, 1953. p. 140-145.

  THE HEAT OF THE DAY

    Sackville-West, Edward. **Inclinations.** London, Secker and Warburg, 1949. p. 95-101.

BRONTË, CHARLOTTE

  JANE EYRE

    Chase, Richard. "The Brontës." **The Kenyon Review** 9:487-506, Autumn, 1947.

    Dry, Florence (Swinton). **The Sources of "Jane Eyre".** Cambridge, W. Heffer, 1940. p. 1-92.

    Hinkley, Laura L. **The Brontës, Charlotte and Emily.** New York, Hastings House, 1945. p. 250-275.

    McCullough, Bruce Welker. **Representative English Novelists: Defoe to Conrad.** New York, Harper, 1946. p. 174-183.

    Scargill, M.H. "All Passion Spent: a Revaluation of **Jane Eyre.**" **University of Toronto Quarterly** 19:120-125, January 1950.

    Tillotson, Kathleen Mary. **Novels of the Eighteen-Forties.** Oxford, Clarendon Press, 1954. p. 286-313.

  THE PROFESSOR

Twentieth Century Criticisms

    Hinkley, Laura L. **The Brontës, Charlotte and Emily.** New York, Hastings House, 1945. p. 231-249.

SHIRLEY

    Hinkley, Laura L. **The Brontës, Charlotte and Emily.** New York, Hastings House, 1945. p. 276-317.

    Korg, Jacob. "The Problem of Unity in **Shirley.**" **Nineteenth-Century Fiction** 12:125-136, September 1957.

VILLETTE

    Falconer, J.A. "**The Professor** and **Villette:** A Study of Development." **English Studies** 9:33-37, April 1927.

BRONTË, EMILY

    WUTHERING HEIGHTS

    Allen, Walter Ernest. **The English Novel; a Short Critical History.** London, Phoenix House, 1954. p. 185-190.

    Allott, Miriam. "**Wuthering Heights:** The Rejection of Heathcliff?" **Essays in Criticism** 8:27-47, January 1958.

    Bald, Marjory Amelia. **Women-Writers of the Nineteenth Century.** Cambridge, Eng., The University Press, 1923. p. 78-88.

    Bradner, Leicester. "The Growth of **Wuthering Heights.**" **PMLA** 48:129-146, March 1933.

    Buckler, William E. "Chapter VII of **Wuthering Heights:** A Key to Interpretation." **Nineteenth-Century Fiction** 7:51-55, June 1952.

    Cecil, Lord David. **Early Victorian Novelists; Essays in Revaluation.** London, Constable, 1934. p. 147-193.

    Chase, Richard. "The Brontës." **Kenyon Review** 9:487-506, Autumn, 1947.

Dry, Mrs. Florence (Swinton). **The Sources of "Wuthering Heights."** Cambridge, Eng., W. Heffer, 1937.

Edgar, Pelham. **The Art of the Novel From 1700 to the Present Time.** New York, Macmillan, 1933. p. 141-145.

Ford, Boris. **"Wuthering Heights".** Scrutiny 7:375-389, March 1939.

Fotheringham, James. "The Work of Emily Brontë and the Brontë Problem." Brontë Society. **Publications** 11:107-134, 1900.

Grabo, Carl Henry. **The Technique of the Novel.** New York, Scribner's, 1928, p. 139-150.

Hinkley, Laura L. **The Brontës, Charlotte and Emily.** New York, Hastings House, 1945. p. 318-343.

Kettle, Arnold. **An Introduction to the English Novel.** London, Hutchinson's, 1951-53. v.1 p.139-155.

Klingopulis, G.D. "The Novel as Dramatic Poem (II): **Wuthering Heights."** Scrutiny 14:269-286, September 1947.

Lehman, B.H. "Of Material, Subject, and Form: **Wuthering Heights."** University of California Publications. **English Studies** 11:3-17, 1955.

McCullough, Bruce Welker. **Representative English Novelists: Defoe to Conrad.** New York, Harper, 1946. p. 185-196.

S., C.P. **The Structure of "Wuthering Heights".** London, L. & Virginia Woolf, 1926. (Hogarth Essays. 19).

Schorer, Mark. "Fiction and the 'analogical matrix'." In John W. Aldridge. **Critiques and Essays on Modern Fiction, 1920-1951.** New York, Ronald Press, 1952. p. 86-91. Also in **Kenyon Review** 11:544-550, Autumn, 1949.

Spark, Muriel. **Emily Brontë, her Life and Work.** London,

Twentieth Century Criticisms

Owen, 1953. p. 232-268.

Van Ghent, Dorothy. **The English Novel.** New York, Rinehart, 1953. p. 153-170.

— — — — —. "The Window Figure and the Two-Children Figure in **Wuthering Heights.**" **Nineteenth-Century Fiction** 7:189-197, December 1952.

Watson, Melvin R. "Tempest in the Soul: The Theme and Structure of Wuthering Heights." **Nineteenth-Century Fiction** 4:87-100, September 1949.

— — — — —. "**Wuthering Heights** and the Critics." **Nineteenth-Century Fiction** 3:243-263, March 1949.

Willis, Irene Cooper. **The Authorship of "Wuthering Heights."** London, Hogarth Press, 1936. p. 11-45.

Worth, George J. "Emily Brontë's Mr. Lockwood." **Nineteenth-Century Fiction** 12:315-320, March 1958.

BUNYAN, JOHN

THE HOLY WAR

Brittain, Vera Mary. **In the Steps of John Bunyan; an Excursion into Puritan England.** London, Rich and Cowan, 1951. (American title: **Valiant Pilgrim**) p. 339-349.

Lindsay, Jack. **John Bunyan, Maker of Myths.** London, Methuen, 1937. p. 212-227.

Sharrock, Roger. **John Bunyan.** London, Hutchinson's University Library, 1954. p. 118-136.

Talon, Henri Antoine. **John Bunyan, the Man and His Works.** (tr. by Barbara Wall) London, Rockliff, 1951. p. 240-256.

Tillyard, Eustace Mandeville Wetenhall. **The English Epic and**

Its Background. New York, Oxford University Press, 1954. p. 397-406.

Tindall, William York. **John Bunyan, Mechanic Preacher.** New York, Columbia University Press, 1934. (Columbia University Studies in English and Comparative Literature no. 119) p. 144-165.

Willcock, Mary Patricia. **Bunyan Calling; a Voice from the Seventeenth Century.** London, Allen & Unwin, 1944. p. 217-228.

THE LIFE AND DEATH OF MR. BADMAN

Dobrée, Bonamy. **Variety of Ways.** Oxford, Clarendon Press, 1932. p. 36-45.

Griffith, Gwilym Oswald. **John Bunyan.** London, Hodder, 1929. p. 245-255.

Hussey, Maurice. "John Bunyan and the Books of God's Judgments." **English** 7:165-167, Spring 1949.

Lindsay, Jack. **John Bunyan, Maker of Myths.** London, Methuen, 1937. p. 203-211.

Sharrock, Roger. **John Bunyan.** London, Hutchinson's University Library, 1954. p. 106-117.

Talon, Henri Antoine. **John Bunyan, the Man and his Works.** (tr. by Barbara Wall) London, Rockliff, 1951. p. 225-239.

Wharey, James Blanton. "Bunyan's Mr. Badman and the Picaresque Novel." University of Texas. **Studies in English.** No. 4 p. 49-61, March 15, 1924.

Willcock, Mary Patricia. **Bunyan Calling; a Voice from the Seventeenth Century.** London, Allen & Unwin, 1944. p. 203-216.

PILGRIM'S PROGRESS

Brittain, Vera Mary. **In the Steps of John Bunyan; an Excursion**

Twentieth Century Criticisms

into Puritan England. London, Rich and Cowan, 1951. (American title: Valiant Pilgrim) p. 298-324.

Firth, Sir Charles Harding. Essays, Historical and Literary. Oxford, Clarendon Press, 1938. p. 129-173.

— — — — —. "John Bunyan." English Association. Leaflet. no. 19, p. 11-26, October, 1911.

Gibson, Daniel, Jr. "On the Genesis of Pilgrim's Progress". Modern Philology 32:365-382, May 1935.

Golder, Harold. "Bunyan's Giant Despair". Journal of English and Germanic Philology. 30:361-378, 1931.

Golder, Harold. "Bunyan and Spenser." PMLA 45:216-237, March 1930.

— — — — —. "Bunyan's Valley of the Shadow." Modern Philology 27:55-72, August, 1929.

Griffith, Gwilym Oswald. John Bunyan. London, Hodder, 1929. p. 220-245.

Hussey, M. "Bunyan's 'Mr. Ignorance!'" Modern Language Review 44:483-489, October, 1949.

Kelman, John. The Road; a Study of John Bunyan's "Pilgrim's Progress." Edinburgh, Oliphant Anderson and Ferrier, 1912.

Lindsay, Jack. John Bunyan, Maker of Myths. London, Methuen, 1937. p. 165-196.

Lowes, John Livingston. Essays in Appreciation. Boston, Houghton Mifflin, 1936. p. 35-74. Also in Lowes, John Livingston. Of Reading Books; Four Essays. London, Constable, 1930. p. 3-44.

Mackail, John William. Studies in Humanism. London, Longmans

Green, 1938. p. 144-168.

Noyes, Alfred. **The Opalescent Parrot.** London, Sheed & Ward, 1929. p. 71-106.

Porter, Arthur. **The Inside of Bunyan's Dream.** London, The Religious Tract Society, 1927.

Sharrock, Roger. **John Bunyan.** London, Hutchinson's University Library, 1954. p. 73-104.

Talon, Henri Antoine. **John Bunyan, the Man and His Works.** (tr. by Barbara Wall) London, Rockliff, 1951. p. 141-224.

Van Ghent, Dorothy. **The English Novel.** New York, Rinehart, 1953. p. 21-32.

Wharey, James Blanton. **A Study of the Sources of Bunyan's Allegories.** Baltimore, J.H. Furst, 1904.

Willcock, Mary Patricia. **Bunyan Calling; a Voice from the Seventeenth Century.** London, Allen & Unwin, 1944. p. 166-202.

Williamson, H.R. "**The Pilgrim's Progress** Reconsidered." **Fortnightly Review** 163:347-352, May 1948.

Wright, Clifford Kent. **Bunyan as a Man of Letters.** Oxford, B.H. Blackwell, 1916. p. 11-18.

BURNEY, FANNY

EVELINA

Montague, Edwine and Louis L. Martz. "Fanny Burney's **Evelina.**" in **The Age of Johnson: Essays Presented to Chauncey Brewster Tinker.** New Haven, Yale University Press, 1949. p. 170-181.

Scrutton, Mary. "Bourgeois Cinderellas." **Twentieth Century** 155:355-360, April 1954.

Twentieth Century Criticisms
BUTLER, SAMUEL

EREWHON

Bekker, William Gerard. **An Historical and Critical Review of Samuel Butler's Literary Works.** Rotterdam, Gedrukt bij Nijgh & Van Ditmar, 1925. p. 107-134.

Cannon, Gilbert. **Samuel Butler; a Critical Study.** London, M. Secker, 1915. p. 25-43.

Cole, George Douglas Howard. **Samuel Butler and "The Way of all Flesh".** London, Home & Van Thal, 1947. p. 80-92.

Harris, John F. **Samuel Butler.** London, G. Richards, 1916. p. 66-88.

Henkin, Leo Justin. **Darwinism in the English Novel, 1860-1910.** New York, Corporate Press, 1940. p. 95-104.

Holt, Lee Elbert. "Samuel Butler's Revisions of **Erewhon.**" Bibliographical Society of America. **Papers** 38:22-38, 1944.

Stillman, Clara Gruening. **Samuel Butler, a Mid-Victorian Modern.** New York, Viking Press, 1932. p. 82-94.

Wilson, Edmund. **The Shores of Light.** New York, Farrar, Straus and Young, 1952. p. 557-565.

— — — — —. **The Triple Thinkers.** London, J. Lehmann, 1952. p. 210-219.

EREWHON REVISITED

Bekker, William Gerard. **An Historical and Critical Review of Samuel Butler's Literary Works.** Rotterdam, Gedrukt bij Nijgh & Van Ditmar, 1925. p. 134-152.

Furbank, Philip Nickolas. **Samuel Butler (1835-1902).** Cambridge University Press, 1948. p. 82-94.

Harris, John F. **Samuel Butler.** London, G. Richards, 1916. p. 89-97.

THE WAY OF ALL FLESH

Bekker, William Gerard. **An Historical and Critical Review of Samuel Butler's Literary Works.** Rotterdam, Gedrukt bij Nijgh & Van Ditmar, 1925. p. 166-187.

Bissell, Claude T. "A Study of The Way of All Flesh." In Herbert J. Davis, ed., **Nineteenth-Century Studies.** Ithaca, N.Y., Cornell University Press, 1940. p. 277-303.

Cannan, Gilbert. **Samuel Butler; a Critical Study.** London, M. Secker, 1915. p. 99-128.

Cole, George Douglas Howard. **Samuel Butler and "The Way of All Flesh."** London, Home & Van Thal, 1947. p. 93-106.

Garnett, Martha (Roscoe). **Samuel Butler and His Family Relations.** London, Dent, 1926. p. 174-195.

Hackett, Francis. **Horizons; a Book of Criticism.** New York, Huebsch, 1919. p. 83-91.

Harris, John F. **Samuel Butler.** London, G. Richards, 1916. p. 216-244.

Henkin, Leo Justin. **Darwinism in the English Novel, 1860-1910.** New York, Corporate Press, 1940. p. 209-217.

Kettle, Arnold. **An Introduction to the English Novel.** London, Hutchinson's, 1951-53. v.2. p. 35-48.

Murry, John Middleton. **Aspects of Literature.** New York, A.A. Knopf, 1920. p. 107-120.

Pritchett, Victor Sawdon. **The Living Novel.** New York, Reynal & Hitchcock, 1947. p. 109-115.

Stillman, Clara Gruening. **Samuel Butler, a Mid-Victorian Modern.**

Twentieth Century Criticisms

>New York, Viking Press, 1932. p. 190-205.

CARROLL, LEWIS

ALICE'S ADVENTURES IN WONDERLAND

>Benardete, Doris. "Alice Among the Professors." **Western Humanities Review** 5:239-247, Summer 1951.

CARY, JOYCE

MISTER JOHNSON

>Kettle, Arnold. **An Introduction to the English Novel.** London, Hutchinson's, 1951-53. v.2 p. 177-184.

COLLINS, WILKIE

ARMADALE

>Ashley, Robert. **Wilkie Collins.** London, Arthur Barker, 1952. p. 84-88.

MAN AND WIFE

>Ashley, Robert. **Wilkie Collins.** London, Arthur Barker, 1952. p. 96-100.

THE MOONSTONE

>Ashley, Robert. **Wilkie Collins.** London, Arthur Barker, 1952. p. 88-96.

>Eliot, T.S. "Wilkie Collins and Dickens." In his **Selected Essays 1917-1932.** London, Faber & Faber, 1932. p. 408-418.

>Milley, H.J.W. "**The Eustace Diamonds** and **The Moonstone.**" **Studies in Philology** 36:651-663, October 1939.

NO NAME

The English Novel

Ashley, Robert. **Wilkie Collins.** London, Arthur Barker, 1952. p. 80-84.

Tillotson, Geoffrey. **Criticism and the Nineteenth Century.** London, Athlone Press, 1951. p. 231-243.

THE WOMAN IN WHITE

Ashley, Robert. **Wilkie Collins.** London, Arthur Barker, 1952. p. 59-70.

Hyder, Clyde K. "Wilkie Collins and **The Woman in White."** **PMLA** 54:297-303, March 1939.

COMPTON-BURNETT, IVY

A FAMILY AND A FORTUNE

Kettle, Arnold. **An Introduction to the English Novel.** London, Hutchinson's, 1951-53. v.2 p. 184-190.

CONRAD, JOSEPH

ALMAYER'S FOLLY

Crankshaw, Edward. **Joseph Conrad; Some Aspects of the Art the Novel.** London, John Lane, 1936. p. 63-87.

Gordan, John Dozier. **Joseph Conrad; the Making of a Novelist.** Cambridge, Mass., Harvard University Press, 1940. p. 112-129.

Tomlinson, H.M. "The Prelude." In George T. Keating. **A Conrad Memorial Library.** Garden City, Doubleday, 1929. p.3-7.

Wiley, Paul L. **Conrad's Measure of Man.** Madison, University of Wisconsin Press, 1954. p. 34-38.

Wright, Walter F. **Romance and Tragedy in Joseph Conrad.** Lincoln, University of Nebraska Press, 1949. p. 55-56, 126-128.

THE ARROW OF GOLD

Twentieth Century Criticisms

    Bendz, Ernst. **Joseph Conrad: An Appreciation.** Gothenburg, Gumbert, 1923. p. 79-84.

    Crankshaw, Edward. **Joseph Conrad; Some Aspects of the Art of the Novel.** London, John Lane, 1936. p.138-145, 192-200.

    Curle, Richard. "**The Arrow of Gold.**" In George T. Keating. **A Conrad Memorial Library.** Garden City, Doubleday, 1929. p. 273-277.

    Mansfield, Katherine. **Novels and Novelists.** Edited by J.M. Murry. New York, Knopf, 1930. p. 60-64.

    Wiley, Paul L. **Conrad's Measure of Man.** Madison, University of Wisconsin Press, 1954. p. 162-173.

    Wright, Walter Francis. **Romance and Tragedy in Joseph Conrad.** Lincoln, University of Nebraska Press, 1949. p. 75-88.

CHANCE

    Beach, Joseph Warren. **The Twentieth Century Novel: Studies in Technique.** New York, Appleton-Century, 1932. p. 337-365.

    Bendz, Ernst. **Joseph Conrad: An Appreciation.** Gothenburg, Gumbert, 1923. p. 67-69.

    Bradbrook, M.C. **Joseph Conrad: Poland's English Genius.** Cambridge University Press, 1942. p. 50-61.

    Coleman, A.P. "Polonisms in Conrad's **Chance.**" **Modern Language Notes** 46:463-468, November 1931.

    Crankshaw, Edward. **Joseph Conrad; Some Aspects of the Art of the Novel.** London, John Lane, 1936. p. 124-133.

    Curle, Richard. **Joseph Conrad: A Study.** London, Kegan Paul, 1914. p. 45-47.

    Follett, Wilson. **Joseph Conrad: A Short Study of His Intellectual and Emotional Attitude Toward His Work and of the**

Chief Characteristics of His Novels. Garden City, Doubleday, 1915. p. 97-100.

Grabo, Carl Henry. **The Technique of the Novel.** New York, Scribner's, 1928. p. 66-71.

Guerard, Albert J. **Joseph Conrad.** New York, New Directions, 1947. p. 48-51.

Harkness, Bruce. "The Epigraph of Conrad's **Chance.**" **Nineteenth Century Fiction** 9:209-222, December 1954.

Haugh, Robert F. "Conrad's **Chance:** Progression D'effet." **Modern Fiction Studies** 1:9-15, February 1955.

Hewitt, Douglas John. **Conrad; a Reassessment.** Cambridge, Bowes & Bowes, 1952. p. 89-102.

Leavis, F.R. **The Great Tradition: George Eliot, Henry James, Joseph Conrad.** London, Chatto & Windus, 1948. p. 222-225.

Megroz, R.L. **Joseph Conrad's Mind and Method: A Study of Personality in Art.** London, Faber, 1931. p. 213-223.

Powys, John Cooper. "Chance" In George T. Keating. **A Conrad Memorial Library.** Garden City, Doubleday, 1929. p. 217-222.

Walpole, Hugh. **Joseph Conrad.** London, Hutchinson, 1929. p. 50-54.

Warner, Oliver. **Joseph Conrad.** London, Longmans, 1951. p. 158-163.

Wiley, Paul L. **Conrad's Measure of Man.** Madison, University of Wisconsin Press, 1954. p. 141-150.

LORD JIM

Allen, Walter Ernest. **Six Great Novelists.** London, H. Hamilton 1955. p. 165-172.

Twentieth Century Criticisms

Bradbrook, M.C. **Joseph Conrad: Poland's English Genius.** Cambridge University Press, 1942. p. 20-27.

Chillag, Charles. "The 'Others' in Conrad's **Lord Jim.**" **English A Analyst** (Northwestern University English Department) No. 21, February 1953.

Crankshaw, Edward. **Joseph Conrad: Some Aspects of the Art of the Novel.** London, John Lane, 1936. p. 50-54.

Curle, Richard. **Joseph Conrad: A Study.** London, Kegan Paul, 1914. p. 33-37.

Day, A. Grove. "Pattern in **Lord Jim.**" College English 13: 396-397, April 1952.

Elphinstone, Petronella. "Tuan Jim." **New Statesman** p. 202-205, August 20, 1932.

Follett, Wilson. **Joseph Conrad: a Short Study of His Intellectual and Emotional Attitude Toward His Work and of the Chief Characteristics of His Novels.** Garden City, N.Y., Doubleday Page, 1915. p. 85-90.

Gordan, John Dozier. **Joseph Conrad; the Making of a Novelist.** Cambridge, Mass., Harvard University Press, 1940. p. 150-173.

— — — — —. "The Rajah Brook and Joseph Conrad." **Studies in Philology** 35:625-633. 1938.

Haugh, Robert F. "Joseph Conrad and Revolution." **College English** 10:273-277, February, 1949.

— — — — —. "The Structure of **Lord Jim.**" College English 13:137-141, December 1951.

Hewitt, Douglas John. **Conrad; a Reassessment.** Cambridge, Bowes & Bowes, 1952. p. 31-49.

Hoffman, Richard. "Proportion and Incident in Joseph Conrad

and Arnold Bennett." **Sewanee Review** 32:79-87, 1924.

McCullough, Bruce Welker. **Representative English Novelists: Defoe to Conrad.** New York, Harper, 1946. p. 342-348.

Morf, Gustav. **The Polish Heritage of Joseph Conrad.** London, S. Low, Marston, 1930. p. 149-166.

Morris, Robert L. "The Classical Reference in Conrad's Fiction." **College English** 7:312-318, March 1946.

Paulding, Gouverneur; Helen MacInnes and Lyman Bryson. "Conrad's **Lord Jim.**" **Invitation to Learning** 2:236-242, Fall 1952.

Powys, T.F. "**Lord Jim.**" In George T. Keating. **A Conrad Memorial Library.** Garden City, Doubleday, 1929. p. 65-70.

Stawell, F. Melian. "Joseph Conrad." English Association. **Essays and Studies** 7:93-96, 1920.

Stegner, Wallace. "Variations on a Theme by Conrad." **Yale Review** 39:512-523, March 1950.

Ure, Peter. "Character and Imagination in Conrad." **Cambridge Journal** 3:733-737, September 1950.

Van Ghent, Dorothy. **The English Novel.** New York, Rinehart, 1953. p. 229-244.

Walpole, Hugh. **Joseph Conrad.** London, Hutchinson, 1929. p. 43-48.

Wiley, Paul L. **Conrad's Measure of Man.** Madison, University of Wisconsin Press, 1954. p. 51-63.

Wright, Walter Francis. **Romance and Tragedy in Joseph Conrad.** Lincoln, University of Nebraska Press, 1949. p. 107-123.

Twentieth Century Criticisms

THE NIGGER OF THE "NARCISSUS"

Bendz, Ernst. **Joseph Conrad: An Appreciation.** Gothenbourg, Gumbert, 1923. p. 46-53.

Davis, Harold E. "Symbolism in **The Nigger of the 'Narcissus'.**" **Twentieth Century Literature** 2:26-29, April 1956.

Follett, Wilson. **Joseph Conrad; a Short Study of his Intellectual and Emotional Attitude Toward his Work and of the Chief Characteristics of his Novels.** Garden City, Doubleday Page, 1915. p. 40-48.

Gordan, John Dozier. **Joseph Conrad; the Making of a Novelist.** Cambridge, Mass., Harvard University Press, 1940. p. 130-150.

Guerard, Albert J. "The Nigger of the 'Narcissus'." **Kenyon Review** 19:205-232, Spring 1957.

Haugh, Robert F. "Death and Consequences: Joseph Conrad's Attitude Towards Fate." **University of Kansas City Review** 18:191-197, Spring 1952.

Miller, James E., "**The Nigger of the 'Narcissus'**: a Re-examination." **PMLA** 66:911-918, December 1951.

Morley, Christopher. "**The Nigger of the 'Narcissus'.**" In George T. Keating. **A Conrad Memorial Library.** Garden City, Doubleday, 1929. p. 28-31.

Mudrick, Marvin. "The Artist's Conscience and **The Nigger of the 'Narcissus'.**" **Nineteenth-Century Fiction** 11:288-297, March 1957.

Watt, Ian. "Conrad Criticism and **The Nigger of the 'Narcissus'.**" **Nineteenth-Century Fiction** 12:257-283, March 1958.

Wiley, Paul L. **Conrad's Measure of Man.** Madison, University of Wisconsin Press, 1954. p. 44-50.

Young, Vernon. "Trial by Water: Joseph Conrad's **The Nigger of the 'Narcissus'.**" **Accent** 12:67-81, Spring 1952.

NOSTROMO

Allen, Walter Ernest. **Six Great Novelists.** London, H. Hamilton, 1955. p. 175-181.

Bendz, Ernst. **Joseph Conrad: An Appreciation.** Gothenburg, Gumbert, 1923. p. 63-67.

Bradbrook, M.C. **Joseph Conrad: Poland's English Genius.** Cambridge University Press, 1942. p. 41-48.

Brewster, Dorothy and Angus Burrell. **Dead Reckonings in Fiction.** New York, Longmans, 1924. p. 101-128. Also in their **Modern Fiction.** New York, Columbia University Press, 1934. p. 69-83.

Brown, E.K. "James and Conrad." **Yale Review** 35:273-277, 1945.

Crankshaw, Edward. **Joseph Conrad; Some Aspects of the Art of the Novel.** London, John Lane, 1936. p. 151-158, 178-191.

Curle, Richard. "The Background of **Nostromo.**" In his **Caravansary and Conversation.** London, Stokes, 1937. p. 207-221.

Edgar, Pelham. **The Art of the Novel from 1700 to the Present Time.** New York, Macmillan, 1933. p. 190-195.

Follett, Wilson. **Joseph Conrad; a Short Study of his Intellectual and Emotional Attitude Toward His Work and of the Chief Characteristics of His Novels.** Garden City, N.Y., Doubleday, Page, 1915. p. 57-64.

Hewitt, Douglas John. **Conrad; a Reassessment.** Cambridge, Bowes & Bowes, 1952. p. 46-69.

Howe, Irving. "Joseph Conrad III. The Political Novels."

Twentieth Century Criticisms

Kenyon Review 16:6-19, Winter 1954.

Kettle, Arnold. **An Introduction to the English Novel.** London, Hutchinson's, 1951-53. v.2 p. 67-81.

Leavis, F.R. "Joseph Conrad." In John W. Aldridge. **Critiques and Essays on Modern Fiction, 1920-1951.** New York, Ronald Press, 1952. p. 120-128. Also in F.R. Leavis. **The Great Tradition.** London, Chatto & Windus, 1948. p. 191-201.

Lynskey, Winifred. "The Role of the Silver in **Nostromo.**" **Modern Fiction Studies** 1:16-21, February 1955.

Megroz, R.L. **Joseph Conrad's Mind and Method: A Study of Personality in Art.** London, Faber, 1931. p. 205-213.

Morf, Gustav. **The Polish Heritage of Joseph Conrad.** London, S. Low, Marston, 1930. p. 127-148.

Stawell, F. Melian. "Joseph Conrad." English Association. **Essays and Studies** 6:105-111, 1920.

Vidan, Ivo. "One Source of Conrad's **Nostromo.**" **Review of English Studies.** New Series 7:287-293, July 1956.

Warner, Oliver. **Joseph Conrad.** London, Longmans, 1951. p. 98-104.

Warren, Robert Penn. "**Nostromo.**" **Sewanee Review** 59:363-391, Summer 1951.

Wiley, Paul L. **Conrad's Measure of Man.** Madison, University of Wisconsin Press, 1954. p. 98-106.

Wright, Walter Francis. **Romance and Tragedy in Joseph Conrad.** Lincoln, University of Nebraska Press, 1949. p. 137-142.

AN OUTCAST OF THE ISLANDS

Clifford, Hugh. "**An Outcast of the Islands.**" In George T.

Keating. **A Conrad Memorial Library.** Garden City, Doubleday, 1929. p. 14-21.

Gordan, John Dozier. **Joseph Conrad: The Making of a Novelist.** Cambridge, Mass., Harvard University Press, 1940. p.189-198.

Wiley, Paul L. **Conrad's Measure of Man.** Madison, University of Wisconsin Press, 1954. p. 39-43.

Young, Vernon. "Lingard's Folly: The Lost Subject." **Kenyon Review** 15:529-536, Autumn 1953.

THE RESCUE

Bendz, Ernst. **Joseph Conrad: An Appreciation.** Gothenburg, Gumbert, 1923. p. 57-62.

Crankshaw, Edward. **Joseph Conrad: Some Aspects of the Art of the Novel.** London, John Lane, 1936. p. 54-62.

Gordan, John Dozier. **Joseph Conrad: The Making of a Novelist.** Cambridge, Mass., Harvard University Press, 1940. p.198-219.

— — — — —. "The Rajah Brooke and Joseph Conrad." **Studies in Philology** 35:619-625, 1938.

Munro, Neil. "The Rescue." In George T. Keating. **A Conrad Memorial Library.** Garden City, Doubleday, 1929. p. 288-293.

Wiley, Paul L. **Conrad's Measure of Man.** Madison, University of Wisconsin Press, 1954. p. 174-187.

THE SECRET AGENT

Bendz, Ernst. **Joseph Conrad: An Appreciation.** Gothenburg, Gumbert, 1923. p. 69-74.

Crankshaw, Edward. **Joseph Conrad; Some Aspects of the Art of the Novel.** London, John Lane, 1936. p. 161-166.

Hagan, John Jr. "The Design of Conrad's **The Secret Agent.**"

Twentieth Century Criticisms

ELH 22:148-164, June 1955.

Hewitt, Douglas. **Conrad: A Reassessment.** Cambridge, Bowes & Bowes, 1952. p. 85-88.

Howe, Irving. "Joseph Conrad: The Political Novels." **Kenyon Review** 16:1-6, Winter 1954.

Leavis, Frank Raymond. **The Great Tradition: George Eliot, Henry James, Joseph Conrad.** London, Chatto, 1948. p.209-219.

Pritchett, V.S. "Conrad: The Exile, the Isolated Man." **New Statesman** 40:72-73, July 15, 1950.

Walpole, Hugh. "The Secret Agent." In George T. Keating. **A Conrad Memorial Library.** Garden City, Doubleday, 1929. p. 159-164.

Warner, Oliver. **Joseph Conrad.** London, Longmans, 1951. p. 104-113.

Wiley, Paul L. **Conrad's Measure of Man.** Madison, University of Wisconsin Press, 1954. p. 107-121.

Wright, Walter Francis. **Romance and Tragedy in Joseph Conrad.** Lincoln, University of Nebraska Press, 1949. p. 175-197.

UNDER WESTERN EYES

Bendz, Ernst. **Joseph Conrad: An Appreciation.** Gothenburg, Gumbert, 1923. p. 74-79.

Canby, Henry Seidel. "**Under Western Eyes.**" In George T. Keating. **A Conrad Memorial Library.** Garden City, Doubleday, 1929. p. 187-193.

Crankshaw, Edward. **Joseph Conrad; Some Aspects of the Art of the Novel.** London, John Lane, 1936. p. 206-215.

Haugh, Robert F. "Joseph Conrad and Revolution." **College**

English 10:273-277, February 1949.

Hewitt, Douglas John. **Conrad; a Reassessment.** Cambridge, Bowes & Bowes, 1952. p. 80-84.

Howe, Irving. "Joseph Conrad. Order and Anarchy: The Political Novels." **Kenyon Review** 15:514-521, Autumn 1953.

Kaye, Julian B., "Conrad's **Under Western Eyes** and Mann's **Doctor Faustus**." **Comparative Literature** 9:60-65, Winter 1957.

Leavis, F.R. **The Great Tradition: George Eliot, Henry James, Joseph Conrad.** London, Chatto & Windus, 1948. p. 219-222.

Pritchett, V.S. **Books in General.** New York, Harcourt, 1953. p. 216-222.

Stawell, F. Melian. "Joseph Conrad." English Association. **Essays and Studies** 6:96-101, 1920.

Warner, Oliver. **Joseph Conrad.** London, Longmans, 1951. p. 113-120.

Wiley, Paul L. **Conrad's Measure of Man.** Madison, University of Wisconsin Press, 1954. p. 122-126.

VICTORY

Bradbrook, M.C. **Joseph Conrad: Poland's English Genius.** Cambridge University Press, 1942. p. 61-67.

de la Mare, Walter. "Conrad's **Victory**." In his **Private View.** London, Faber and Faber, 1953. p. 19-22.

Follett, Wilson. **Joseph Conrad; a Short Study of his Intellectual and Emotional Attitude Toward his Work and of the Chief Characteristics of his Novels.** Garden City, N.Y., Doubleday, Page, 1915. p. 14-28.

Gatch, Katherine H. "Conrad's Axel." **Studies in Philology**

Twentieth Century Criticisms

48:98-106, 1951.

Hewitt, Douglas John. **Conrad; a Reassessment.** Cambridge, Bowes & Bowes, 1952. p. 103-111.

Leavis, Frank Raymond. **The Great Tradition: George Eliot, Henry James, Joseph Conrad.** London, Chatto, 1948. p. 201-209.

Machen, Arthur. "**Victory.**" In George T. Keating. **A Conrad Memorial Library.** Garden City, Doubleday, 1929. p. 245-249.

Morf, Gustav. **The Polish Heritage of Joseph Conrad.** London, Sampson Low, 1930. p. 176-180.

Morris, Robert L. "The Classical Reference in Conrad's Fiction." **College English** 7:312-318, March 1946.

Raphael, Alice Pearl. **Goethe, the Challenger.** New York, J. Cape and R. Ballou, 1932. p. 41-83.

Stallman, Robert Wooster. "The Structure and Symbolism of Conrad's **Victory.**" **Western Review** 13:146-157, Spring 1949.

Warner, Oliver. **Joseph Conrad.** London, Longmans 1951. p.120-126.

Wiley, Paul L. **Conrad's Measure of Man.** Madison, University of Wisconsin Press, 1954. p. 151-157.

Wright, Walter Francis. **Romance and Tragedy in Joseph Conrad.** Lincoln, University of Nebraska Press, 1949. p. 101-106.

DAY, THOMAS

SANDFORD AND MERTON

Pritchett, Victor Sawdon. **The Living Novel.** New York, Reynal & Hitchcock, 1947. p. 44-49.

DEFOE, DANIEL

CAPTAIN SINGLETON

Secord, Arthur Wellesley. **Studies in the Narrative Method of Defoe.** Urbana, Ill., University of Illinois, 1924. (University of Illinois Studies in Language and Literature, v.9) p. 112-164.

MOLL FLANDERS

MacCarthy, Sir Desmond. **Criticism.** London, Putnam, 1932. p. 216-222.

McCullough, Bruce Welker. **Representative English Novelists: Defoe to Conrad.** New York, Harper, 1946. p. 10-22.

McKillop, Alan Dugald. **The Early Masters of English Fiction.** Lawrence, University of Kansas Press, 1956. p. 28-33.

Quennell, P.C. **The Singular Preference.** London, Collins, 1952. p. 126-131.

Rodway, A.E. "**Moll Flanders** and **Manon Lescaut.**" **Essays in Criticism** 3:303-320, July 1953.

Sen, C. **Daniel Defoe, His Mind and Art.** Calcutta, University of Calcutta, 1948. p. 208-213.

Van Ghent, Dorothy. **The English Novel.** New York, Rinehart, 1953. p. 33-43.

Watt, Ian. **The Rise of the Novel; Studies in Defoe, Richardson and Fielding.** London, Chatto and Windus, 1957. p. 93-134.

ROBINSON CRUSOE

Benjamin, Edwin B. "Symbolic Elements in **Robinson Crusoe.**" **Philological Quarterly** 30:206-211, April 1951.

Häusermann, Hans W. "Aspects of Life and Thought in **Robinson Crusoe.**" **Review of English Studies** 11:299-312, 439-456,

Twentieth Century Criticisms

July, October 1935.

Kronenberger, Louis. **The Republic of Letters; Essays on Various Writers.** New York, Knopf, 1955. p. 50-55.

Laird, John. **Philosophical Incursions Into English Literature.** Cambridge, University Press, 1946. p. 21-33.

McKillop, Alan Dugald. **The Early Masters of English Fiction.** Lawrence, University of Kansas Press, 1956. p. 20-25.

Robins, H.F. "How Smart Was Robinson Crusoe?" **PMLA** 67: 782-789, September, 1952.

Secord, Arthur Wellesley. **Studies in the Narrative Method of Defoe.** Urbana, Ill., University of Illinois, 1924. (University of Illinois Studies in Language and Literature v.9) p. 21-111.

Sen, C. **Daniel Defoe, His Mind and Art.** Calcutta, University of Calcutta, 1948. p. 234-256.

Swallow, Alan. "Defoe and the Art of Fiction." **Western Humanities Review** 4:133-134, Spring 1950.

Watson, Francis. **Daniel Defoe.** London, Longman, Green, 1952. p. 6-18.

Watt, Ian. **The Rise of the Novel; Studies in Defoe, Richardson and Fielding.** London, Chatto and Windus, 1957. p. 60-92.

— — — — —. **"Robinson Crusoe as a Myth." Essays in Criticism** 1:95-119, April 1951.

Woolf, Virginia (Stephen). **The Common Reader.** Second Series. London, L. & Virginia Woolf at the Hogarth Press, 1932. p. 51-58.

Wright, Thomas. **The Life of Daniel Defoe.** Bi-centenary ed. London, C.J. Farncombe, 1931. p. 239-251.

ROXANA

McKillop, Alan Dugald. **The Early Masters of English Fiction.** Lawrence, University of Kansas Press, 1956. p. 35-38.

Peterson, Spiro. "The Matrimonial Theme of Defoe's **Roxana.**" **PMLA** 70:166-191, March 1955.

Raleigh, John Henry. "Style and Structure and Their Import in Defoe's **Roxana.**" **University of Kansas City Review** 20:128-135, Winter 1953.

Sen, C. **Daniel Defoe, His Mind and Art.** Calcutta, University of Calcutta, 1948. p. 213-221.

DICKENS, CHARLES

BARNABY RUDGE

Butt, John and Kathleen Tillotson. **Dickens at Work.** London, Methuen, 1957. p. 76-89.

Chesterton, Gilbert Keith. **Criticisms and Appreciations of the Works of Charles Dickens.** London, Dent, 1933. p. 65-75.

Gissing, George Robert. **Critical Studies of the Works of Charles Dickens.** New York, Greenberg, 1924. p. 103-118.

Johnson, Edgar. **Charles Dickens. His Tragedy and Triumph.** New York, Simon and Schuster, 1952. p. 329-337.

Wilson, Edmund. **The Wound and the Bow.** New York, Oxford University Press, 1947. p. 14-23.

BLEAK HOUSE

Butt, John. "**Bleak House** in the Context of 1851." **Nineteenth-Century Fiction** 10:1-21, June 1955.

— — — — —. **Dickens at Work.** London, Methuen, 1957. p. 177-200.

Twentieth Century Criticisms

    Chesterton, Gilbert Keith. **Criticisms and Appreciations of the Works of Charles Dickens.** London, Dent, 1933. p. 148-159.

    Crompton, Louis. "Satire and Symbolism in **Bleak House.**" **Nineteenth-Century Fiction** 12:284-303, March 1958.

    Gissing, George Robert. **Critical Studies of the Works of Charles Dickens.** New York, Greenberg, 1924. p. 136-150.

    Johnson, Edgar. "**Bleak House,** The Anatomy of Society." **Nineteenth-Century Fiction** 7:73-89, September 1952.

    — — — — —. **Charles Dickens, His Tragedy and Triumph.** New York, Simon and Schuster, 1952. p. 762-782.

    Whipple, Edwin Percy. **Charles Dickens, The Man and His Work.** Boston, Houghton Mifflin, 1912. v.2 p. 55-91.

    Wilson, Edmund. **The Wound and the Bow.** New York, Oxford University Press, 1947. p. 35-43.

DAVID COPPERFIELD

    Brown, E.K. "**David Copperfield.**" **Yale Review** 37:651-666, Summer 1948.

    Butt, John and Kathleen Tillotson. **Dickens at Work.** London, Methuen, 1957. p. 114-176.

    Chesterton, Gilbert Keith. **Criticisms and Appreciations of the Works of Charles Dickens.** London, Dent, 1933. p. 129-139.

    Johnson, Edgar. **Charles Dickens, His Tragedy and Triumph.** New York, Simon and Schuster, 1952. p. 677-700.

    McCullough, Bruce Welker. **Representative English Novelists: Defoe to Conrad.** New York, Harper, 1946. p. 139-151.

    Needham, Gwendolyn B. "The Undisciplined Heart of David Copperfield." **Nineteenth-Century Fiction** 9:81-107, September 1954.

Priestley, John Boynton. **The English Comic Characters.** London, J. Lane, 1928. p. 241-276.

Strong, Leonard Alfred George. **Personal Remarks.** London, P. Nevill, 1953. p. 103-122.

Tedlock, E.W., Jr. "Kafka's Imitation of **David Copperfield.**" **Comparative Literature** 7:52-62, Winter 1955.

Whipple, Edwin Percy. **Charles Dickens; the Man and His Work.** Boston, Houghton Mifflin, 1912. v.2 p. 3-54.

Woolf, Virginia. "**David Copperfield.**" In her **The Moment and Other Essays** London, Hogarth, 1947. p. 65-69.

DOMBEY AND SON

Butt, John and Kathleen Tillotson. **Dickens at Work.** London, Methuen, 1957. p. 90-113.

— — — — —. "Dickens at Work on **Dombey and Son.**" English Association. **Essays and Studies.** v.4 new ser: 70-93, 1951.

Chesterton, Gilbert Keith. **Criticisms and Appreciations of the Works of Charles Dickens.** London, Dent, 1933. p. 114-128.

Edgar, Pelham. **The Art of the Novel from 1700 to the Present Time.** New York, Macmillan, 1933. p. 118-122.

Gissing, George Robert. **Critical Studies of the Works of Charles Dickens.** New York, Greenberg, 1924. p. 89-102.

Johnson, Edgar. **Charles Dickens, His Tragedy and Triumph.** New York, Simon and Schuster, 1952. p. 626-643.

Sackville-West, Edward. **Inclinations.** London, Secker and Warburg, 1949. p. 20-26.

Tillotson, Kathleen Mary. **Novels of the Eighteen-Forties.** Oxford, Clarendon Press, 1954. p. 157-201.

Twentieth Century Criticisms

    Whipple, Edwin Percy. **Charles Dickens; the Man and His Work.** Boston, Houghton Mifflin, 1912. v.1 p. 241-286.

GREAT EXPECTATIONS

    Connolly, Thomas E. "Technique in **Great Expectations**." **Philological Quarterly** 34:48-55, January 1955.

    Friedman, Norman. "Versions of Form in Fiction - - **Great Expectations** and **The Great Gatsby**." **Accent** 14:246-264. Autumn 1954.

    Hagan, John H. Jr. "The Poor Labyrinth: The Theme of Social Injustice in Dickens' **Great Expectations**." **Nineteenth-Century Fiction** 9:169-178, December 1954.

    — — — — —. "Structural Patterns in Dickens' **Great Expectations**." **ELH** 21:54-66, March 1954.

    House, Humphrey. **All in Due Time.** London, Rupert Hart-Davis, 1955. p. 201-220.

    Johnson, Edgar. **Charles Dickens, His Tragedy and Triumph.** New York, Simon and Schuster, 1952. p. 982-994.

    Shaw, George Bernard. "**Great Expectations**." In Van Wyck Brooks and Others. **A Book of Prefaces.** New York, The Limited Editions Club, 1941. p. 29-43.

    Strange, G. Robert. "Expectations Well Lost: Dickens' Fable for His Time." **College English** 16:9-17, October 1954.

    Van Ghent, Dorothy. **The English Novel.** New York, Rinehart, 1953. p. 125-138.

    Whipple, Edwin Percy. **Charles Dickens, the Man and His Work.** Boston, Houghton Mifflin, 1912. v.2 p. 201-231.

HARD TIMES

    Butt, John and Kathleen Tillotson. **Dickens at Work.** London, Methuen, 1957. p. 201-221.

Chesterton, Gilbert Keith. **Criticisms and Appreciations of the Works of Charles Dickens.** London, Dent, 1933. p. 169-177.

Johnson, Edgar. **Charles Dickens, His Tragedy and Triumph.** New York, Simon and Schuster, 1952. p. 801-819.

Leavis, Frank Raymond. **The Great Tradition: George Eliot, Henry James, Joseph Conrad.** London, Chatto, 1948. p. 227-248.

— — — — —. "The Novel as Dramatic Poem (i): **Hard Times.**" **Scrutiny** 14:185-203, Spring 1947.

Waldock, A.J.A. "The Status of **Hard Times.**" **Southerly** 9: 33-39, 1948.

Whipple, Edwin Percy. **Charles Dickens; the Man and His Work.** Boston, Houghton Mifflin, 1912. v.2 p. 92-115.

LITTLE DORRIT

Butt, John and Kathleen Tillotson. **Dickens at Work.** London, Methuen, 1957. p. 222-233.

Chesterton, Gilbert Keith. **Criticisms and Appreciations of the Works of Charles Dickens.** London, Dent, 1933. p. 178-187.

Johnson, Edgar. **Charles Dickens, His Tragedy and Triumph.** New York, Simon and Schuster, 1952. p. 883-903.

Trilling, Lionel. "**Little Dorrit.**" **Kenyon Review** 15:577-590, Autumn 1953. Also in Lionel Trilling. **The Opposing Self; Nine Essays in Criticism.** New York, Viking Press, 1955. p.50-65.

Whipple, Edwin Percy. **Charles Dickens; the Man and His Work.** Boston, Houghton Mifflin, 1912. v.2 p. 116-179.

Wilson, Edmund. **Axel's Castle; a Study in the Imaginative Literature of 1870-1930.** New York, Scribner, 1939. p. 44-59.

MARTIN CHUZZLEWIT

Benjamin, Edwin B. "The Structure of **Martin Chuzzlewit.**"

Twentieth Century Criticisms

    Philological Quarterly 34:39-47, January 1955.

    Chesterton, Gilbert Keith. **Criticisms and Appreciations of the Works of Charles Dickens.** London, Dent, 1933. p. 90-102.

    Gissing, George Robert. **Critical Studies of the Works of Charles Dickens.** New York, Greenberg, 1924. p. 72-88.

    Johnson, Edgar. **Charles Dickens, His Tragedy and Triumph.** New York, Simon and Schuster, 1952. p. 469-483.

    Nicholas, H.G. "Martin Chuzzlewit and the America of 1842." **History Today** 1:58-61, March 1951.

    Stone, Harry. "Dickens' Use of his American Experiences in Martin Chuzzlewit." **PMLA** 72:464-478, June 1957.

    Whipple, Edwin Percy. **Charles Dickens; the Man and His Work.** Boston, Houghton Mifflin, 1912. v.1 p. 186-240.

THE MYSTERY OF EDWIN DROOD

    Baker, Richard Merriam. **The Drood Murder Case; Five Studies in Dickens' "Edwin Drood".** Berkeley, University of California Press, 1951.

    — — — — —. "Who Was Dick Datchery?" **Nineteenth-Century Fiction** 2:201-222, March 1948. 3:35-53, June 1948.

    Johnson, Edgar. **Charles Dickens, His Tragedy and Triumph.** New York, Simon and Schuster, 1952. p. 1115-1126.

    Pritchett, Victor Sawdon. **The Living Novel.** New York, Reynal & Hitchcock, 1947. p. 83-88.

    Whipple, Edwin Percy. **Charles Dickens; the Man and His Work.** Boston, Houghton Mifflin, 1912. p. 300-354.

    Wilson, Edmund. **The Wound and the Bow.** New York, Oxford University Press, 1947. p. 83-104.

NICHOLAS NICKLEBY

Adrian, Arthur A. "**Nicholas Nickleby** and Educational Reform." **Nineteenth-Century Fiction** 4:237-241, December 1949.

Chesterton, Gilbert Keith. **Criticisms and Appreciations of the Works of Charles Dickens.** London, Dent, 1933. p. 26-37.

Gissing, George Robert. **Critical Studies of the Works of Charles Dickens.** New York, Greenberg, 1924. p. 58-71.

Johnson, Edgar. **Charles Dickens, His Tragedy and Triumph.** New York, Simon and Schuster, 1952. p. 283-291.

Whipple, Edwin Percy. **Charles Dickens; the Man and His Work.** Boston, Houghton Mifflin, 1912. v.1 p. 72-99.

OLD CURIOSITY SHOP

Chesterton, Gilbert Keith. **Criticisms and Appreciations of the Works of Charles Dickens.** London, Dent, 1933. p. 50-64.

Gissing, George Robert. **Critical Studies of the Works of Charles Dickens.** New York, Greenberg, 1924. p. 119-135.

Johnson, Edgar. **Charles Dickens, His Tragedy and Triumph.** New York, Simon and Schuster, 1952. p. 319-329.

Priestley, John Boynton. **The English Comic Characters.** London, J. Lane, 1928. p. 224-240.

Whipple, Edwin Percy. **Charles Dickens; the Man and His Work.** Boston, Houghton Mifflin, 1912. v.1 p. 100-127.

OLIVER TWIST

Chesterton, Gilbert Keith. **Criticisms and Appreciations of the Works of Charles Dickens.** London, Dent, 1933. p. 38-49.

Eoff, Sherman. "**Oliver Twist** and the Spanish Picaresque Novel." **Studies in Philology** 54:440-447, July 1957.

Twentieth Century Criticisms

>Gissing, George Robert. **Critical Studies of the Works of Charles Dickens.** New York, Greenberg, 1924. p. 43-57.

>Greene, Graham. **The Lost Childhood and Other Essays.** London, Eyre and Spottiswoode, 1951, p. 51-57.

>House, Humphrey. **All in Due Time.** London, Rupert Hart-Davis, 1955. p. 190-200.

>Johnson, Edgar. **Charles Dickens, His Tragedy and Triumph.** New York, Simon and Schuster, 1952. p. 273-283.

>Kettle, Arnold. **An Introduction to the English Novel.** London, Hutchinson's, 1951-53. v.1 p. 123-138.

>Lucas, Alec. "Oliver Twist and the Newgate Novel." **Dalhousie Review** 34:381-387, Spring 1954.

>Pritchett, Victor Sawdon. **Books in General.** London, Chatto, 1953. p. 191-196.

>Whipple, Edwin Percy. **Charles Dickens; the Man and His Work.** Boston, Houghton Mifflin, 1912. v.1 p. 54-71.

OUR MUTUAL FRIEND

>Chesterton, Gilbert Keith. **Criticisms and Appreciations of the Works of Charles Dickens.** London, Dent, 1933. p. 207-217.

>Johnson, Edgar. **Charles Dickens, His Tragedy and Triumph.** New York, Simon and Schuster, 1952. p. 1022-1045.

>Morse, R. "**Our Mutual Friend.**" Partisan Review 16:277-289, March 1949.

>Quennell, P.C. "**Our Mutual Friend.**" In his **The Singular Preference.** London, Collins, 1952. p. 152-158.

>Whipple, Edwin Percy. **Charles Dickens; the Man and His Work.** Boston, Houghton Mifflin, 1912. v.2 p. 232-275.

Wilson, Edmund. **The Wound and the Bow.** New York, Oxford University Press, 1947. p. 74-83.

PICKWICK PAPERS

Butt, John and Kathleen Tillotson. **Dickens at Work.** London, Methuen, 1957. p. 62-75.

Chesterton, Gilbert Keith. **Charles Dickens.** London, Methuen, 1936. p. 51-71.

— — — — —. **Criticisms and Appreciations of the Works of Charles Dickens.** London, Dent, 1933. p. 13-25.

Fadiman, Clifton. "Pickwick Live Forever." **Atlantic Monthly** 184:23-29, December 1949.

Gissing, George Robert. **Critical Studies of the Works of Charles Dickens.** New York, Greenberg, 1924. p. 30-43.

Johnson, Edgar. **Charles Dickens, His Tragedy and Triumph.** New York, Simon and Schuster, 1952. p. 157-175.

Maclean, H.N. "Mr. Pickwick and the Seven Deadly Sins." **Nineteenth-Century Fiction** 8:198-212, December 1953.

Priestley, John Boynton. **The English Comic Characters.** London, J. Lane, 1928. p. 198-223.

A TALE OF TWO CITIES

Johnson, Edgar. **Charles Dickens, His Tragedy and Triumph.** New York, Simon and Schuster, 1952. p. 972-982.

Whipple, Edwin Percy. **Charles Dickens; the Man and His Work.** Boston, Houghton Mifflin, 1912. v.2 p. 180-200.

ELIOT, GEORGE

ADAM BEDE

Bennett, Joan (Frankau). **George Eliot, Her Mind and Her Art.**

Twentieth Century Criticisms

Cambridge, University Press, 1948. p. 102-114.

Bullett, Gerald William. **George Eliot, Her Life and Books.** London, Collins, 1947. p. 171-179.

Creeger, George R. "An Interpretation of **Adam Bede.**" **ELH** 23:218-238, September 1956.

Diekhoff, John S. "The Happy Ending of **Adam Bede.**" **ELH** 3:221-227, September 1936.

Haldane, Elizabeth Sandison. **George Eliot and Her Times; a Victorian Study.** New York, Appleton, 1927. p. 143-154.

Hutton, Richard Holt. **Essays on Some of the Modern Guides of English Thought in Matters of Faith.** London, Macmillan, 1914. p. 179-194.

Pritchett, Victor Sawdon. **The Living Novel.** New York, Reynal & Hitchcock, 1947. p. 91-96.

Stephen, Sir Leslie. **George Eliot.** London, Macmillan, 1902. p. 64-85.

Van Ghent, Dorothy. **The English Novel.** New York, Rinehart, 1953. p. 171-181.

DANIEL DERONDA

Bennett, Joan (Frankau). **George Eliot, Her Mind and Her Art.** Cambridge, University Press, 1948. p. 181-196.

Bullett, Gerald William. **George Eliot, Her Life and Books.** London, Collins, 1947. p. 204-214.

Haldane, Elizabeth Sandison. **George Eliot and Her Times: a Victorian Study.** New York, Appleton, 1927. p. 262-272.

Hardy, Barbara. "Imagery in George Eliot's Last Novels." **MLR** 50:11-14, January 1955.

Leavis, F.R. "George Eliot (IV): **Daniel Deronda** and **The Portrait of a Lady.**" **Scrutiny** 14:102-131, December 1946.

— — — — —. **The Great Tradition: George Eliot, Henry James, Joseph Conrad.** London, Chatto, 1948. p. 79-125.

Stephen, Sir Leslie. **George Eliot.** London, Macmillan, 1902. p. 185-191.

Thale, Jerome. "River Imagery in **Daniel Deronda.**" **Nineteenth-Century Fiction** 8:300-306, March 1954.

FELIX HOLT

Bennett, Joan (Frankau). **George Eliot, Her Mind and Her Art.** Cambridge, University Press, 1948. p. 152-159.

Haldane, Elizabeth Sandison. **George Eliot and Her Times: a Victorian Study.** New York, Appleton, 1927. p. 229-240.

Hanson, Lawrence. **Marian Evans and George Eliot.** London, Oxford University Press, 1952. p. 255-261.

Leavis, Frank Raymond. **The Great Tradition: George Eliot, Henry James, Joseph Conrad.** London, Chatto, 1948. p. 50-61.

Speare, Morris Edmund. **The Political Novel.** New York, Oxford University Press, 1924. p. 221-236.

Stephen, Sir Leslie. **George Eliot.** London, Macmillan, 1902. p. 143-157.

MIDDLEMARCH

Allen, Walter Ernest. **The English Novel; a Short Critical History.** London, Phoenix House, 1954. p. 219-223.

Beaty, Jerome. "Visions and Revisions: Chapter LXXXI of **Middlemarch.**" **PMLA** 72:662-679, September 1957.

Bennett, Joan (Frankau). **George Eliot, Her Mind and Her Art.**

Twentieth Century Criticisms

Cambridge, University Press, 1948. p. 160-180.

Bullett, Gerald William. **George Eliot, Her Life and Books.** London, Collins, 1947. p. 215-229.

Haldane, Elizabeth Sandison. **George Eliot and Her Times; a Victorian Study.** New York, Appleton, 1927. p. 245-257.

Hardy, Barbara. "Imagery in George Eliot's Last Novels." **MLR** 50:6-11, January 1955.

Hutton, Richard Holt. **Essays on Some of the Modern Guides of English Thought in Matters of Faith.** London, Macmillan, 1914. p. 208-246.

James, Henry. "George Eliot's Middlemarch." **Nineteenth-Century Fiction** 8:161-170, December 1953.

Kettle, Arnold. **An Introduction to the English Novel.** London, Hutchinson's, 1951-53. v.1 p. 171-190.

Leavis, Frank Raymond. **The Great Tradition: George Eliot, Henry James, Joseph Conrad.** London, Chatto, 1948. p. 61-79.

McCullough, Bruce Welker. **Representative English Novelists: Defoe to Conrad.** New York, Harper, 1946. p. 204-214.

Pritchett, Victor Sawdon. **The Living Novel.** New York, Reynal & Hitchcock, 1947. p. 96-102.

Sackville-West, Edward. **Inclinations.** London, Secker and Warburg, 1949. p. 27-32.

Schorer, Mark. "Fiction and the 'analogical matrix'. In John W. Aldridge. **Critiques and Essays on Modern Fiction, 1920-1951.** New York, Ronald Press, 1952. p. 91-97. Also in **Kenyon Review** 11:550-559, Autumn 1949.

Steiner, F. George. "A Preface to **Middlemarch.**" **Nineteenth-Century Fiction.** 9:262-279, March 1955.

Stephen, Sir Leslie. **George Eliot.** London, Macmillan, 1902. p. 172-184.

THE MILL ON THE FLOSS

Bennett, Joan (Frankau). **George Eliot, Her Mind and Her Art.** Cambridge, University Press, 1948. p. 115-130.

Bullett, Gerald William. **George Eliot, Her Life and Books.** London, Collins, 1947. p. 181-190.

Haldane, Elizabeth Sandison. **George Eliot and Her Times; a Victorian Study.** New York, Appleton, 1927. p. 161-173.

Hanson, Lawrence. **Marian Evans and George Eliot.** London, Oxford University Press, 1952. p. 220-227.

Leavis, Frank Raymond. **The Great Tradition: George Eliot, Henry James, Joseph Conrad.** London, Chatto, 1948. p. 38-46.

Steinhoff, William R. "Intent and Fullfillment in the Ending of **The Mill on the Floss.**" University of California Publications. **English Studies** 11:231-251, 1955.

Stephen, Sir Leslie. **George Eliot.** London, Macmillan, 1902. p. 86-104.

Thale, Jerome. "Image and Theme: **The Mill on the Floss.**" **University of Kansas City Review** 23:227-234, Spring 1957.

ROMOLA

Bennett, Joan (Frankau). **George Eliot, Her Mind and Her Art.** Cambridge, University Press, 1948. p. 139-151.

Haldane, Elizabeth Sandison. **George Eliot and Her Times: a Victorian Study.** New York, Appleton, 1927. p. 196-214.

Hutton, Richard Holt. **Essays on Some of the Modern Guides of English Thought in Matters of Faith.** London, Macmillan, 1914. p. 196-208.

Twentieth Century Criticisms

> Stephen, Sir Leslie. **George Eliot.** London, Macmillan, 1902. p. 122-142.

SILAS MARNER

> Bennett, Joan (Frankau). **George Eliot, Her Mind and Her Art.** Cambridge, University Press, 1948. p. 131-138.
>
> Haldane, Elizabeth Sandison. **George Eliot and Her Times: a Victorian Study.** New York, Appleton, 1927. p. 181-190.
>
> Stephen, Sir Leslie. **George Eliot.** London, Macmillan, 1902. p. 105-111.
>
> Thale, Jerome. "George Eliot's Fable for Her Times." **College English** 19:141-146, January 1958.

THE SPANISH GYPSY

> Stephen, Sir Leslie. **George Eliot.** London, Macmillan, 1902. p. 158-171.

FIELDING, HENRY

AMELIA

> Cross, Wilbur Lucius. **The History of Henry Fielding.** New Haven, Yale University Press, 1928. v.2 p. 301-356.
>
> Dobson, Henry Austin. **Fielding.** London, Macmillan, 1907. p. 151-161.
>
> Dudden, Frederick Homes. **Henry Fielding: His Life, Works and Times.** Oxford, Clarendon Press, 1952. v.2 p. 797-885.
>
> Jenkins, Elizabeth. **Henry Fielding.** London, Home & Van Thal 1947. p. 82-90.
>
> McKillop, Alan Dugald. **The Early Masters of English Fiction.** Lawrence, University of Kansas Press, 1956. p. 136-145.

Sherburn, George. "Fielding's **Amelia:** an Interpretation." In Richard Charles Boys. **Studies in the Literature of the Augustan Age.** Ann Arbor, Mich., Distributed for the Augustan Reprint Society by the George Wahr Pub. Co., 1952. p. 267-280. Also in **ELH** 3:1-14, March 1936.

JONATHAN WILD

Benerji, Hiran Kumar. **Henry Fielding, Playwright, Journalist and Master of the Art of Fiction.** Oxford, Blackwell, 1929. p. 151-166.

Digeon, Aurélieu. **The Novels of Fielding.** London, Routledge, 1925. p. 91-128.

Dudden, Frederick Homes. **Henry Fielding: His Life, Works, and Times.** Oxford, Clarendon Press, 1952. v.1 p. 449-501.

Irwin, William Robert. **The Making of "Jonathan Wild."** New York, Columbia University Press, 1941. (Columbia University Studies in English and Comparative Literature, no. 153).

Kettle, Arnold. **An Introduction to the English Novel.** London, Hutchinson's, 1951-53. v.1 p. 45-51.

Kronenberger, Louis. **The Republic of Letters; Essays on Various Writers.** New York, Knopf, 1955. p. 81-88.

McKillop, Alan Dugald. **The Early Masters of English Fiction.** Lawrence, University of Kansas Press, 1956. p. 114-118.

Shea, Bernard. "Machiavelli and Fielding's **Jonathan Wild.**" **PMLA** 72:55-73, March 1957.

Wendt, Allan. "The Moral Allegory of **Jonathan Wild.**" **ELH** 24:306-320, December 1957.

JOSEPH ANDREWS

Benerji, Hiran Kumar. **Henry Fielding, Playwright, Journalist**

Twentieth Century Criticisms

and Master of the Art of Fiction. Oxford, Blackwell, 1929. p. 110-133.

Bissell, Frederick Olds. **Fielding's Theory of the Novel.** Ithaca, New York, Cornell University Press, 1933. p. 24-37, 67-74.

Cauthen, I.B. "Fielding's Digressions in **Joseph Andrews.**" **College English** 17:379-382, April 1956.

Cross, Wilbur Lucius. **The History of Henry Fielding.** New Haven, Yale University Press, 1928. v.1 p. 314-359.

Digeon, Aurélieu. **The Novels of Fielding.** London, Routledge, 1925. p. 39-90.

Dobson, Henry Austin. **Fielding.** London, Macmillan, 1907. p. 73-88.

Dudden, Frederick Homes. **Henry Fielding: His Life, Works, and Times.** Oxford, Clarendon Press, 1952. v.1 p. 327-392.

Jenkins, Elizabeth. **Henry Fielding.** London, Home & Van Thal, 1947. p. 31-42.

Kettle, Arnold. **An Introduction to the English Novel.** London, Hutchinson's, 1951-53. v.1 p. 72-77.

McKillop, Alan Dugald. **The Early Masters of English Fiction.** Lawrence, University of Kansas Press, 1956. p. 100-114.

Priestley, John Boynton. **The English Comic Characters.** London, J. Lane, 1928. p. 106-127.

Spilka, Mark. "Comic Resolution in Fielding's **Joseph Andrews.**" **College English** 15:11-19, October 1953.

Thornbury, Ethel Margaret. **Henry Fielding's Theory of the Comic Prose Epic.** Madison, 1931. (University of Wisconsin Studies in Language and Literature no. 30) p. 95-111.

SHAMELA

Shepperson, Archibald Bolling. **The Novel in Motley, a History of the Burlesque Novel in English.** Cambridge, Harvard University Press, 1936. p. 19-28.

TOM JONES

Banerji, Hiran Kumar. **Henry Fielding, Playwright, Journalist and Master of the Art of Fiction.** Oxford, Blackwell, 1929. p. 194-215.

Bissell, Frederick Olds. **Fielding's Theory of the Novel.** Ithaca, New York, Cornell University Press, 1933. p. 38-66, 74-80.

Carver, Wayne. "The Worlds of Tom and Tristram." **Western Humanities Review** 12:67-74, Winter 1958.

Crane, Ronald Salmon. "The Concept of Plot and the Plot of Tom Jones." In Ronald Salmon Crane. ed. **Critics and Criticisms Ancient and Modern.** Chicago, University of Chicago Press, 1952. p. 616-647. Reprinted with alterations and additions from **Journal of General Education** 4:112-30, 1950.

Cross, Wilbur Lucius. **The History of Henry Fielding.** New Haven, Yale University Press, 1928. v.2 p. 158-222.

Digeon, Aurélieu. **The Novels of Fielding.** London, Routledge, 1925. p. 129-193.

Dobson, Henry Austin. **Fielding.** London, Macmillan, 1907. p. 121-144.

Dudden, Frederick Homes. **Henry Fielding: His Life, Works and Times.** Oxford, Clarendon Press, 1952. v.2 p. 583-732.

Edgar, Pelham. **The Art of the Novel from 1700 to the Present Time.** New York, Macmillan, 1933. p. 59-67.

Jenkins, Elizabeth. **Henry Fielding.** London, Home & Van Thal,

Twentieth Century Criticisms

    1947. p. 57-76.

    Kettle, Arnold. **An Introduction to the English Novel.** London, Hutchinson's, 1951-53. v.1 p. 76-81.

    Kronenberger, Louis. **The Republic of Letters; Essays on Various Writers.** New York, Knopf, 1955. p. 74-80.

    McCullough, Bruce Welker. **Representative English Novelists: Defoe to Conrad.** New York, Harper, 1946. p. 45-57.

    McKillop, Alan Dugald. **The Early Masters of English Fiction.** Lawrence, University of Kansas Press, 1956. p. 118-136.

    Priestley, John Boynton. "Tom Jones." In Van Wyck Brook and others. **A Book of Prefaces.** New York, The Limited Editions Club, 1941. p. 48-53.

    Thornbury, Ethel Margaret. **Henry Fielding's Theory of the Comic Prose Epic.** Madison, 1931. (University of Wisconsin Studies in Language and Literature no. 30) p. 112-131.

    Van Ghent, Dorothy. **The English Novel.** New York, Rinehart, 1953. p. 65-81.

    Watt, Ian. **The Rise of the Novel; Studies in Defoe, Richardson, and Fielding.** London, Chatto and Windus, 1957. p. 260-289.

FORD, FORD MADOX

    THE GOOD SOLDIER

    Gose, Elliott B., Jr. "The Strange Irregular Rhythm: An Analysis of **The Good Soldier.**" PMLA 72:494-509, June 1957.

    Kenner, Hugh. "Conrad and Ford: The Artistic Conscience." **Shenandoah** 3:53-55, Summer 1952.

    Macauley, Robie. "The Good Ford." **Kenyon Review** 11:270-277, Spring 1949.

    Schorer, Mark. "The Good Novelist in **The Good Soldier.**" **Horizon** 20:132-138, August 1949.

PARADE'S END

Tobyansen, John R. "**Parade's End.**" **Shenandoah** 1:29-36, Winter 1950.

FORSTER, E.M.

HOWARD'S END

Benson, Alice R. "E.M. Forster's Dialectic: **Howard's End.**" **Modern Fiction Studies** 1:17-22, November 1955.

Johnstone, John Keith. **The Bloomsbury Group; a Study of E.M. Forster, Lytton Strachey, Virginia Woolf, and their Circle.** London, Secker & Warburg, 1954. p. 201-230.

Macaulay, Rose. **The Writings of E.M. Forster.** London, Hogarth Press, 1938. p. 98-127.

Savage, Derek S. **The Withered Branch; Six Studies in the Modern Novel.** London, Eyre & Spottiswoode, 1950. p. 57-67.

Trilling, Lionel. **E.M. Forster.** Norfolk, Conn., New Directions, 1943. p. 113-135.

THE LONGEST JOURNEY

Harvey, John. "Imagination and Moral Theme in E.M. Forster's **The Longest Journey. Essays in Criticism** 6:418-433, 1956.

Johnstone, John Keith. **The Bloomsbury Group; a study of E.M. Forster, Lytton Strachey, Virginia Woolf, and their Circle.** London, Secker & Warburg, 1954. p. 176-189.

Macaulay, Rose. **The Writings of E.M. Forster.** London, Hogarth Press, 1938. p. 46-65.

Savage, Derek S. **The Withered Branch; Six Studies in the Modern Novel.** London, Eyre & Spottiswoode, 1950. p. 50-57.

Twentieth Century Criticisms

Trilling, Lionel. **E.M. Forster.** Norfolk, Conn., New Directions, 1943. p. 76-96.

A PASSAGE TO INDIA

Allen, Glen O. "Structure, Symbol, Theme in E.M. Forster's **A Passage to India.**" PMLA 80:934-954, December 1955.

Brower, Reuben Arthur. **The Fields of Light.** New York, Oxford University Press, 1951. p. 182-198.

Brown, Edward Killoran. **Rhythm in the Novel.** Toronto, University of Toronto Press, 1950. p. 89-115.

Henderson, Philip. **The Novel Today; Studies in Contemporary Attitudes.** London, Lane, 1936. p. 91-96.

Johnstone, John Keith. **The Bloomsbury Group; a Study of E.M. Forster, Lytton Strachey, Virginia Woolf, and their Circle.** London, Secker & Warburg, 1954. p. 231-266.

Kettle, Arnold. **An Introduction to the English Novel.** London, Hutchinson's, 1951-53. v.2 p. 152-163.

Macaulay, Rose. **The Writings of E.M. Forster.** London, Hogarth Press, 1938. p. 176-203.

Maclean, Hugh. "The Structure of **A Passage to India.**" **University of Toronto Quarterly** 22:157-171, January 1953.

Stewart, Douglas Alexander. **The Flesh and the Spirit, an Outlook on Literature.** Sydney, Angus and Robertson, 1948. p.17-24.

Trilling, Lionel. **E.M. Forster.** Norfolk, Conn., New Directions, 1943. p. 136-161.

White, Gertrude M. "**A Passage to India:** Analysis and Revaluation." **PMLA** 68:641-657, September 1953.

A ROOM WITH A VIEW

> Johnstone, John Keith. **The Bloomsbury Group; a Study of E.M. Forster, Lytton Strachey, Virginia Woolf, and their Circle.** London, Secker & Warburg, 1954. p. 191-200.
>
> Macaulay, Rose. **The Writings of E.M. Forster.** London, Hogarth Press, 1938. p. 78-97.
>
> Trilling, Lionel. **E.M. Forster.** Norfolk, Conn., New Directions, 1943. p. 97-112.

WHERE ANGELS FEAR TO TREAD

> Johnstone, John Keith. **The Bloomsbury Group; a Study of E.M. Forster, Lytton Strachey, Virginia Woolf, and their Circle.** London, Secker & Warburg, 1954. p. 161-175.
>
> Macaulay, Rose. **The Writings of E.M. Forster.** London, Hogarth Press, 1938. p. 35-45.
>
> Trilling, Lionel. **E.M. Forster.** Norfolk, Conn., New Directions, 1943. p. 57-75.

GALSWORTHY, JOHN

THE FORSYTE SAGA

> Beach, Joseph Warren. **The Twentieth Century Novel; Studies in Technique.** New York, The Century Co., 1932. p. 249-262.
>
> Croman, Natalie. **John Galsworthy, a Study in Continuity and Contrast.** Cambridge, Mass., Harvard University Press, 1933. p. 9-51.
>
> Cross, Wilbur. "The Forsytes." **Yale Review** 19:527-550, March 1930.
>
> McCullough, Bruce Welker. **Representative English Novelists: Defoe to Conrad.** New York, Harper, 1946. p. 326-335.

Twentieth Century Criticisms

FRATERNITY

Harkness, Bruce. "Conrad on Galsworthy: The Time Scheme of **Fraternity."** Modern Fiction Studies 1:12-18, May 1955.

THE MAN OF PROPERTY

Chevrillon, Andre. **Three Studies in English Literature: Kipling, Galsworthy, Shakespeare.** From the French by Florence Simmonds. New York, Doubleday, Page, 1923. p. 160-196.

Kettle, Arnold. **An Introduction to the English Novel.** London, Hutchinson's, 1951-53. v.2 p. 95-100.

GASCOIGNE, GEORGE

ADVENTURES OF MASTER F.J.

Bradner, Leicester. "The First English Novel." **PMLA** 45: 543-552, June 1930.

GASKELL, ELIZABETH

CRANFORD

Sanders, Gerald De Witt. **Elizabeth Gaskell.** New Haven, Yale University Press, 1929. p. 36-46.

MARY BARTON

Ffrench, Yvonne. **Mrs. Gaskell.** London, Home & Van Thal, 1949. p. 21-28.

Hopkins, Annette Brown. **Elizabeth Gaskell.** London, J. Lehmann, 1952. p. 74-79.

— — — — —. "**Mary Barton:** a Victorian Best Seller." **Nineteenth-Century Fiction.** 3:1-18, June 1948.

Sanders, Gerald De Witt. **Elizabeth Gaskell.** New Haven, Yale

University Press, 1929. p. 15-29.

Tillotson, Kathleen Mary. **Novels of the Eighteen-Forties.** Oxford, Clarendon Press, 1954. p. 202-223.

NORTH AND SOUTH

Hopkins, Annette Brown. **Elizabeth Gaskell.** London, J. Lehmann, 1952. p. 139-143.

Sanders, Gerald De Witt. **Elizabeth Gaskell.** New Haven, Yale University Press, 1929. p. 64-76.

RUTH

Ffrench, Yvonne. **Mrs. Gaskell.** London, Home & Van Thal, 1949. p. 51-57.

Hopkins, Annette Brown. **Elizabeth Gaskell.** London, J. Lehmann, 1952. p. 119-134.

Sanders, Gerald De Witt. **Elizabeth Gaskell.** New Haven, Yale University Press, 1929. p. 47-58.

SYLVIA'S LOVERS

Ffrench, Yvonne. **Mrs. Gaskell.** London, Home & Van Thal, 1949. p. 83-92.

Hopkins, Annette Brown. **Elizabeth Gaskell.** London, J. Lehmann, 1952. p. 261-272.

Sanders, Gerald De Witt. **Elizabeth Gaskell.** New Haven, Yale University Press, 1929. p. 114-128.

WIVES AND DAUGHTERS

Hopkins, Annette Brown. **Elizabeth Gaskell.** London, J. Lehmann, 1952. p. 278-296.

Sanders, Gerald De Witt. **Elizabeth Gaskell.** New Haven, Yale

Twentieth Century Criticisms

    University Press, 1929. p. 129-139.

GISSING, GEORGE

    BORN IN EXILE

        Swinnerton, Frank Arthur. **George Gissing, a Critical Study.** London, Secker, 1912. p. 98-104.

    DEMOS

        Donnelly, Mabel Collins. **George Gissing, Grave Comedian.** Cambridge, Harvard University Press, 1954. p. 109-114.

    ISABEL CLARENDON

        Donnelly, Mabel Collins. **George Gissing, Grave Comedian.** Cambridge, Harvard University Press, 1954. p. 101-106.

    THE NETHER WORLD

        Swinnerton, Frank Arthur. **George Gissing, a Critical Study.** London, Secker, 1912. p. 72-76.

    NEW GRUB STREET

        Donnelly, Mabel Collins. **George Gissing, Grave Comedian.** Cambridge, Harvard University Press, 1954. p. 156-161.

        Swinnerton, Frank Arthur. **George Gissing, a Critical Study.** London, Secker, 1912. p. 92-98.

    THYRZA

        Donnelly, Mabel Collins. **George Gissing, Grave Comedian.** Cambridge, Harvard University Press, 1954. p. 114-118.

        Swinnerton, Frank Arthur. **George Gissing, a Critical Study.** London, Secker, 1912. p. 64-72.

THE UNCLASSED

    Donnelly, Mabel Collins. **George Gissing, Grave Comedian.**
Cambridge, Harvard University Press, 1954. p. 70-74.

THE WHIRLPOOL

    Donnelly, Mabel Collins. **George Gissing, Grave Comedian.**
Cambridge, Harvard University Press, 1954. p. 179-183.

WORKERS IN THE DAWN

    Donnelly, Mabel Collins. **George Gissing, Grave Comedian.**
Cambridge, Harvard University Press, 1954. p. 65-70.

    Swinnerton, Frank Arthur. **George Gissing, a Critical Study.**
London, Secker, 1912. p. 46-52.

GODWIN, WILLIAM

CALEB WILLIAMS

    Fleisher, David. **William Godwin.** London, Allen & Unwin.
1951. p. 25-28.

    Furbank, P.N. "Godwin's Novels." **Essays in Criticism** 5:
214-220, July 1955.

    Monro, D. **Godwin's Moral Philosophy.** London, Oxford University Press, 1953. p. 86-98.

    Stephen, Leslie. "William Godwin's Novels." In his **Studies of a Biographer.** New York, Putnam's, 1907. v.3 p. p.140-143.

    Woodcock, George. **William Godwin.** London, Porcupine Press, 1946. p. 117-122.

FLEETWOOD

    Allen, B. Sprague. "William Godwin as a Sentimentalist."
PMLA 33:23-27, 1918.

Twentieth Century Criticisms

ST. LEON

Allen, B. Sprague. "William Godwin as a Sentimentalist." **PMLA** 33:16-23, 1918.

Monro, D. **Godwin's Moral Philosophy.** London, Oxford University Press, 1953. p. 99-108.

Stephen, Leslie. "William Godwin's Novels." In his **Studies of a Biographer.** New York, Putnam's, 1907. v.3, p. 140-143.

GOLDSMITH, OLIVER

THE VICAR OF WAKEFIELD

Saintsbury, George Edward Bateman. **A Saintsbury Miscellany.** New York, Oxford University Press, 1947. p. 165-174.

GREEN, HENRY

PARTY GOING

Kettle, Arnold. **An Introduction to the English Novel.** London, Hutchinson's, 1951-53. v.2 p.191-195.

LOVING

Hall, James. "The Fiction of Henry Greene (sic): Paradoxes of Pleasure-and-Pain." **Kenyon Review** 19:76-88, Winter 1957.

GREENE, GRAHAM

BRIGHTON ROCK

Allott, Kenneth and Miriam Farris (Allott). **The Art of Graham Greene.** London, Hamish Hamilton, 1951. p. 147-160.

Braybrooke, Neville. "Graham Greene, a Pioneer Novelist." **College English** 12:4-6, October 1950.

DeVitis, A.A. "Allegory in **Brighton Rock.**" Modern Fiction

Studies 3:216-224, Autumn 1957.

Ellis, William D. Jr. "The Grand Theme of Graham Greene." **Southwest Review** 41:245-250, Summer 1956.

Haber, Herbert R. "The Two Worlds of Graham Greene." **Modern Fiction Studies** 3:257-264, Autumn 1957.

Lewis, R.W.B. "The 'Trilogy' of Graham Greene." **Modern Fiction Studies** 3:198-203, Autumn 1957.

McGowan, F.A. "Symbolism in **Brighton Rock**." **Renascence** 8:25-35, Autumn 1955.

Mesnet, Marie Béatrice. **Graham Greene and the Heart of the Matter, an Essay.** London, Cresset Press, 1954. p. 13-19, 48-55, 84-86.

Traversi, Derek. "Graham Greene." **Twentieth Century** 149: 237-240, 1951.

Wyndham, Francis. **Graham Greene.** London, Longmans, 1955. p. 15-16. (Bibliographical Series of Supplements to **British Book News** on Writers and Their Work, No. 67).

CONFIDENTIAL AGENT

Allott, Kenneth and Miriam Farris (Allott). **The Art of Graham Greene.** London, Hamish Hamilton, 1951. p. 139-147.

THE END OF THE AFFAIR

Arnold, G.L. "Adam's Tree." **Twentieth Century** 154:337-342, October 1951.

Bogan, Louise. "Good Beyond Evil." **New Republic** 125: 29-30, December 10, 1951.

Braybrooke, Neville. "Graham Greene and the Double Man: an Approach to **The End of the Affair**." **Dublin Review** No. 455,

Twentieth Century Criticisms

    p. 61-73, First Quarter 1952.

    Lees, F.N. "Graham Greene: a Comment." **Scrutiny** 19:40-42, October 1952.

    Spier, Ursula. "Melodrama in Graham Greene's **The End of the Affair**." **Modern Fiction Studies** 3:235-240, Autumn 1957.

THE HEART OF THE MATTER

    Allott, Kenneth and Miriam Farris (Allott). **The Art of Graham Greene.** London, Hamish Hamilton, 1951. p. 214-244.

    Gorden, Caroline. "Some Readings and Misreadings." **Sewanee Review** 61:393-396, July-September 1953.

    Howes, Jane. "Out of Pit." **Catholic World** 171:36-40, April 1950.

    Jefferson, Mary Evelyn. "**The Heart of the Matter**: the Responsible Man." **Carolina Quarterly** 9:23-31, Summer 1957.

    Kettle, Arnold. **An Introduction to the English Novel.** London, Hutchinson's, 1951-53. v.2 p. 171-177.

    Lees, F.N., "Graham Greene: a Comment." **Scrutiny** 19:36-40, October 1952.

    Lewis, R.W.B. "The 'Trilogy' of Graham Greene." **Modern Fiction Studies** 3:211-215, Autumn 1957.

    Mesnet, Marie Béatrice. **Graham Greene and the Heart of the Matter, an Essay.** London, Cresset Press, 1954. p. 28-34, 61-68, 86-89.

    Moré, Marcel. "The Two Holocausts of Scobie." **Cross Currents** 1:44-63, 1951.

    O'Donnell, Donat. **Maria Cross.** New York, Oxford University Press, 1952. p. 63-91.

Traversi, Derek. "Graham Greene." **Twentieth Century** 149: 323-328, 1951.

Waugh, Evelyn. "Felix Culpa?" **Commweal** 48:322-325, July 19, 1948.

Wyndham, Francis. **Graham Greene.** London, Longmans, 1955. p. 20-23. (Bibliographical Series of Supplements to **British Book News** on Writers and Their Work, No. 67).

Zabel, Morton Dauwen. "Graham Greene: The Best and the Worst." In his **Craft and Character in Modern Fiction.** New York, Viking, 1957. p. 290-293.

IT'S A BATTLEFIELD

Allott, Kenneth and Miriam Farris (Allott). **The Art of Graham Greene.** London, Hamish Hamilton, 1951. p. 85-100.

Braybrooke, Neville. "Graham Greene, a Pioneer Novelist." **College English** 12:3-4, October 1950.

THE MAN WITHIN

Allott, Kenneth and Miriam Farris (Allott). **The Art of Graham Greene.** London, Hamish Hamilton, 1951. p. 51-60.

Lewis, R.W.B. "The Fiction of Graham Greene: Between the Horror and the Glory." **Kenyon Review** 19:62-65, Winter 1957.

THE MINISTRY OF FEAR

Allott, Kenneth and Miriam Farris (Allott). **The Art of Graham Greene.** London, Hamish Hamilton, 1951. p. 193-214.

Auden, W.H. "The Heresy of Our Time." **Renascence** 1:23-24, Spring 1949.

THE POWER AND THE GLORY

Allen, Walter Ernest. "Graham Greene." In Denys Val Baker,

Twentieth Century Criticisms

ed. **Writers of To-day.** London, Sidgwick, 1946.

— — — — —. **Reading a Novel.** London, Phoenix House, 1949. p. 34-39.

Allott, Kenneth and Miriam Farris (Allott). **The Art of Graham Greene.** London, Hamish Hamilton, 1951. p. 173-193.

Haber, Herbert R. "The Two Worlds of Graham Greene." **Modern Fiction Studies** 3:264-268, Autumn 1957.

Hoggart, Richard. "The Force of Caricature: Aspects of the Art of Graham Greene with Particular Reference to **The Power and the Glory.**" **Essays in Criticism** 3:447-462, October 1953.

Lees, F.N. "Graham Greene: a Comment." **Scrutiny** 19:32-36, October 1952.

Lewis, R.W.B. "The 'Trilogy' of Graham Greene." **Modern Fiction Studies** 3:203-210, Autumn 1957.

Mauriac, Francois. **Great Men.** London, Rockcliff, 1952. p. 117-121.

Mesnet, Marie Béatrice. **Graham Greene and the Heart of the Matter, an Essay.** London, Cresset Press, 1954. p. 19-28, 56-60, 89-92.

O'Faolain, Sean. "Graham Greene: I Suffer; Therefore, I am." In his **The Vanishing Hero: Studies in Novelists of the Twenties.** London, Eyre and Spottiswoode, 1956. p. 92-95.

Patten, Karl. "The Structure of **The Power and the Glory.**" **Modern Fiction Studies** 3:225-234, Autumn 1957.

Traversi, Derek. "Graham Greene." **Twentieth Century** 149:319-323, 1951.

Woodcock, George. "Mexico and the English Novelists." **Western Review** 21:29-32, Autumn 1956.

THE QUIET AMERICAN

Elistratova, Anna. "Graham Greene and His New Novel." **Soviet Literature** 8:149-155, 1956.

Evans, Robert O. "Existentialism in Graham Greene's **The Quiet American.**" **Modern Fiction Studies** 3:241-248, Autumn 1957.

Freedman, Ralph. "Novel of Contention: **The Quiet American.**" **Western Review** 21:76-81, Autumn 1956.

Lewis, R.W.B. "The Fiction of Graham Greene: Between the Horror and the Glory." **Kenyon Review** 19:56-60, Winter 1957.

Rahv, Philip. "Wicked American Innocence." **Commentary** 21: 488-490, May 1956.

Trilling, Diana, and Philip Rahv. "America and **The Quiet American.**" **Commentary** 22:66-71, July 1956.

RUMOUR AT NIGHTFALL

Allott, Kenneth and Miriam Farris (Allott). **The Art of Graham Greene.** London, Hamish Hamilton, 1951. p. 60-71.

STAMBOUL TRAIN

Allott, Kenneth and Miriam Farris (Allott). **The Art of Graham Greene.** London, Hamish Hamilton, 1951. p. 79-85.

THE THIRD MAN

Alloway, Lawrence. "Symbolism in **The Third Man.**" **World Review** p. 57-60, March 1950.

HARDY, THOMAS

DESPERATE REMEDIES

Beach, Joseph Warren. **The Technique of Thomas Hardy.**

Twentieth Century Criticisms

Chicago, University of Chicago Press, 1922. p. 23-35.

FAR FROM THE MADDING CROWD

Beach, Joseph Warren. **The Technique of Thomas Hardy.** Chicago, University of Chicago Press, 1922. p. 45-79.

Brown, Douglas. **Thomas Hardy.** London, Longmans, 1954. p. 48-55.

Chew, Samuel Daggett. **Thomas Hardy, Poet and Novelist.** New York, Knopf, 1929. p. 33-38.

Grimsditch, Herbert B. **Character and Environment in the Novels of Thomas Hardy.** London, H.F. & G. Witherby, 1925. p. 160-166.

Webster, Harvey Curtis. **On a Darkling Plain.** Chicago, University of Chicago Press. 1947. p. 107-113.

Williams, Randall. **The Wessex Novels of Thomas Hardy.** London, Dent, 1924. p. 72-78.

THE HAND OF ETHELBERTA

Webster, Harvey Curtis. **On a Darkling Plain.** Chicago, University of Chicago, 1947. p. 113-118.

JUDE THE OBSCURE

Abercrombie, Lascelles. **Thomas Hardy, a Critical Study.** London, Secker, 1912. p. 152-169.

Beach, Joseph Warren. **The Technique of Thomas Hardy.** Chicago, University of Chicago Press, 1922. p. 218-244.

Chase, Mary Ellen. **Thomas Hardy from Serial to Novel.** Minneapolis, University of Minneapolis Press, 1927. p. 115-177.

Chew, Samuel Daggett. **Thomas Hardy, Poet and Novelist.** New York, Knopf, 1929. p. 67-74.

Duffin, Henry Charles. **Thomas Hardy; a Study of the Wessex Novels.** Manchester, University Press, 1921. p. 159-188.

Guerard, Albert J. **Thomas Hardy; the Novels and the Stories.** Cambridge, Harvard University Press, 1949. p. 152-157.

Holland, Norman. "Jude the Obscure: Hardy's Symbolic Indictment of Christianity." **Nineteenth-Century Fiction** 9:50-60, June 1954.

Hoopes, K.R. "Illusion and Reality in **Jude the Obscure.**" **Nineteenth-Century Fiction** 12:154-157, September 1957.

Mizener, Arthur. "**Jude the Obscure** as a Tragedy." **Southern Review** 6:193-213, Summer 1940.

Nevinson, Henry Woodd. **Thomas Hardy.** London, G. Allen, 1941. p. 31-36.

Slack, Robert C. "The Text of Hardy's **Jude the Obscure.**" **Nineteenth-Century Fiction** 11:261-275, March 1957.

Webster, Harvey Curtis. **On a Darkling Plain.** Chicago, University of Chicago Press, 1947. p. 183-189.

Williams, Randall. **The Wessex Novels of Thomas Hardy.** London, Dent, 1924. p. 27-35.

THE MAYOR OF CASTERBRIDGE

Baker, James R. "Thematic Ambiguity in **The Mayor of Casterbridge.**" **Twentieth Century Literature** 1:13-16, April 1955.

Beach, Joseph Warren. **The Technique of Thomas Hardy.** Chicago, University of Chicago Press, 1922. p. 134-157.

Braybrooke, Patrick. **Thomas Hardy and His Philosophy.** London, C.W. Daniel, 1928. p. 36-45.

Brogan, Howard O. "'Visible Essences' in **The Mayor of Caster-**

Twentieth Century Criticisms

bridge." **ELH** 17:307-323, December 1950.

Brown, Douglas. **Thomas Hardy.** London, Longmans, 1954. p. 63-70.

Chase, Mary Ellen. **Thomas Hardy from Serial to Novel.** Minneapolis, University of Minneapolis Press, 1927. p. 15-65.

Dike, D.A. "A Modern Oedipus: The Mayor of Casterbridge." **Essays in Criticism.** 2:169-179, April 1952.

Duffin, Henry Charles. **Thomas Hardy; a Study of the Wessex Novels.** Manchester, University Press, 1921. p. 99-106.

Gardner, W.H. "Some thoughts on The Mayor of Casterbridge." English Association. **Pamphlet** no. 77, November 1930.

Guerard, Albert J. **Thomas Hardy; the Novels and the Stories.** Cambrdige, Harvard University Press, 1949. p. 146-152.

Haber, Grace Stevenson. "Echoes from Carlyle's **Goethe's Helena** in The Mayor of Casterbridge." **Nineteenth-Century Fiction** 12:89-90, June 1957.

Moynahan, Julian. "**The Mayor of Casterbridge** and the **Old Testament's** first Book of Samuel: A Study of Some Literary Relationships." **PMLA** 71:118-130, March 1956.

Webster, Harvey Curtis. **On a Darkling Plain.** Chicago, University of Chicago Press, 1947. p. 147-152.

A PAIR OF BLUE EYES

Beach, Joseph Warren. **The Technique of Thomas Hardy.** Chicago, University of Chicago Press, 1922. p. 36-44.

Chew, Samuel Daggett. **Thomas Hardy, Poet and Novelist.** New York, Knopf, 1929. p. 27-33.

Grimsditch, Herbert B. **Character and Environment in the Novels**

The English Novel of Thomas Hardy. London, H.F. & G. Witherby, 1925. p. 107-116.

Webster, Harvey Curtis. **On a Darkling Plain.** Chicago, University of Chicago Press, 1947. p. 101-107.

THE RETURN OF THE NATIVE

Allen, Walter Ernest. **The English Novel; a Short Critical History.** London, Phoenix House, 1954. p. 235-240.

Beach, Joseph Warren. **The Technique of Thomas Hardy.** Chicago, University of Chicago Press, 1922. p. 80-105.

Braybrooke, Patrick. **Thomas Hardy and His Philosophy.** London, C.W. Daniel, 1928. p. 24-35.

Brown, Douglas. **Thomas Hardy.** London, Longmans, 1954. p. 55-63.

Duffin, Henry Charles. **Thomas Hardy; a Study of the Wessex Novels.** Manchester, University Press, 1921. p. 106-113.

Goldberg, M.A. "Hardy's Double-Visioned Universe." **Essays in Criticism** 7:374-382, 1957.

Grabo, Carl Henry. **The Technique of the Novel.** New York, Scribner's, 1928. p. 113-133

Grimsditch, Herbert B. **Character and Environment in the Novels of Thomas Hardy.** London, H.F. & G. Witherby, 1925. p.53-62.

Grove, Frederick Philip. "Thomas Hardy; a Critical Examination of a Typical Novel and His Shorter Poems." **University of Toronto Quarterly.** 1:492-499, July 1932.

McCullough, Bruce Welker. **Representative English Novelists: Defoe to Conrad.** New York, Harper, 1946. p. 237-249.

Stallman, Robert Wooster. "Hardy's Hour-Glass Novel." **Sewanee Review.** 55:283-296, April-June 1947.

Twentieth Century Criticisms

    Webster, Harvey Curtis. **On a Darkling Plain.** Chicago, University of Chicago Press, 1947. p. 118-125.

    Williams, Randall. **The Wessex Novels of Thomas Hardy.** London, Dent, 1924. p. 9-13.

TESS OF THE D'URBERVILLES

    Abercrombie, Lascelles. **Thomas Hardy, a Critical Study.** London, Secker, 1912. p. 129-152.

    Beach, Joseph Warren. **The Technique of Thomas Hardy.** Chicago, University of Chicago Press, 1922. p. 180-217.

    Braybrooke, Patrick. **Thomas Hardy and His Philosophy.** London, C.W. Daniel, 1928. p. 46-62.

    Brown, Douglas. **Thomas Hardy.** London, Longmans, 1954. p. 89-98.

    Chase, Mary Ellen. **Thomas Hardy from Serial to Novel.** Minneapolis, University of Minneapolis Press, 1927. p. 69-112.

    Chew, Samuel Daggett. **Thomas Hardy, Poet and Novelist.** New York, Knopf, 1929. p. 59-65.

    Duffin, Henry Charles. **Thomas Hardy; a Study of the Wessex Novels.** Manchester, University Press, 1921. p. 145-158.

    Guerard, Albert J. **Thomas Hardy; the Novels and the Stories.** Cambridge, Harvard University Press, 1949. p. 109-114.

    Kettle, Arnold. **An Introduction to the English Novel.** London, Hutchinson's, 1951-53. v.2 p. 49-62.

    Linn, James Weber. **A Foreword to Fiction.** New York, Appleton-Century-Croft, 1935. p. 122-136.

    Van Ghent, Dorothy. **The English Novel.** New York, Rinehart, 1953. p. 195-209.

Webster, Harvey Curtis. **On a Darkling Plain.** Chicago, University of Chicago Press, 1947. p. 173-180.

Williams, Randall. **The Wessex Novels of Thomas Hardy.** London, Dent, 1924. p. 20-27.

TWO IN A TOWER

Webster, Harvey Curtis. **On a Darkling Plain.** Chicago, University of Chicago Press, 1947. p. 143-146.

THE WOODLANDERS

Beach, Joseph Warren. **The Technique of Thomas Hardy.** Chicago, University of Chicago, 1922. p. 158-176.

Brown, Douglas. **Thomas Hardy.** London, Longmans, 1954. p. 70-89.

Edgar, Pelham. **The Art of the Novel from 1700 to the Present Time.** New York, Macmillan, 1933. p. 165-171.

Matchett, William H. "The Woodlanders, or Realism in Sheep's Clothing." **Nineteenth-Century Fiction** 9:241-261, March 1955.

Meibergen, C.R. "The Woodlanders." **Englische Studien** 51:226-247, October 1917.

Webster, Harvey Curtis. **On a Darkling Plain.** Chicago, University of Chicago Press, 1947. p. 166-173.

HOLCROFT, THOMAS

ALWYN

Stallbaumer, Virgil R. "Thomas Holcroft as a Novelist." **ELH** 15:196-201, September 1948.

ANNA ST. IVES

Stallbaumer, Virgil R. "Thomas Holcroft as a Novelist." **ELH**

Twentieth Century Criticisms

15:204-210, September 1948.

HUGH TREVOR

Stallbaumer, Virgil R. "Thomas Holcroft as a Novelist." **ELH** 15:210-216, September 1948.

HUXLEY, ALDOUS

AFTER MANY A SUMMER

Baker, Howard. "In Praise of the Novel: the Fiction of Huxley, Steinbeck and Others." **Southern Review** 5:780-786, Spring 1940.

Savage, D.S. "Aldous Huxley and the Dissociation of Personality." In John W. Aldridge. **Critiques and Essays on Modern Fiction, 1920-1951.** New York, Ronald Press, 1952. p.357-361. Also in D.S. Savage. **The Withered Branch.** Eyre and Spottiswoode, 1950. And in **Sewanee Review,** Autumn 1947.

ANTIC HAY

Daiches, David. **The Novel and the Modern World.** Chicago, University of Chicago Press, 1939. p. 192-197.

Henderson, Alexander. **Aldous Huxley.** New York, Harper, 1936. p. 135-141.

BRAVE NEW WORLD

Curle, Adam. "Huxley's Brave New World." **New Statesman and Nation** 49:508-509, April 9, 1955.

Henderson, Alexander. **Aldous Huxley.** New York, Harper, 1936. p. 87-111.

Woodcock, George. "Utopias in Negative." **Sewanee Review** 64:81-97, Winter 1956.

CROME YELLOW

Henderson, Alexander. **Aldous Huxley.** New York, Harper, 1936. p. 128-135.

EYELESS IN GAZA

Bentley, Phyllis. "The Structure of **Eyeless in Gaza.**" **The English Journal** (College Edition) 26:127-132, February 1937.

Savage, D.S. "Aldous Huxley and the Dissociation of Personality." In John W. Aldridge. **Critiques and Essays on Modern Fiction, 1920-1951.** New York, Ronald Press, 1952. p. 350-355. Also in D.S. Savage. **The Withered Branch.** Eyre and Spottiswoode, 1950. And in **Sewanee Review** Autumn, 1947.

POINT COUNTERPOINT

Beach, Joseph Warren. **The Twentieth Century Novel; Studies in Technique.** New York, The Century Co., 1932. p. 458-469.

Brewster, Dorothy. **Modern Fiction.** New York, Columbia University Press, 1934. p. 248-256.

Daiches, David. **The Novel and the Modern World.** Chicago, University of Chicago Press, 1939. p. 203-206.

Henderson, Alexander. **Aldous Huxley.** New York, Harper, 1936. p. 40-87.

Henderson, Philip. **The Novel Today; Studies in Contemporary Attitudes.** London, Lane, 1936. p. 120-129.

MacCarthy, Sir Desmond. **Criticism.** London, Putnam, 1932. p. 240-246.

Muller, Herbert Joseph. **Modern Fiction.** New York, Funk & Wagnals, 1937. p. 385-390.

THOSE BARREN LEAVES

Henderson, Alexander. **Aldous Huxley.** New York, Harper, 1936. p. 111-128.

Savage, Derek S. **The Withered Branch; Six Studies in the Modern Novel.** London, Eyre & Spottiswoode, 1950. p. 134-140.

Twentieth Century Criticisms

TIME MUST HAVE A STOP

Wilson, Edmund. **Classics and Commercials.** New York, Farrar, Straus, 1950. p. 209-214.

JOHNSON, SAMUEL

RASSELAS

Conant, Martha Pike. **The Oriental Tale in England in the Eighteenth Century.** New York, Columbia University Press, 1908. (Columbia University Studies in English and Comparative Literature no. 17) p. 140-154.

Kolb, Gwin J. "The Structure of **Rasselas.**" PMLA 66:698-717, September 1951.

Lascelles, Mary. "**Rasselas** Reconsidered." English Association. **Essays and Studies** 4 new ser.: 37-52, 1951.

Lunn, Hugh Kingsmill. **Samuel Johnson.** London, A Barker, 1933. p. 109-114.

Whitley, Alvin. "The Comedy of **Rasselas.**" ELH 23:48-70, March 1956.

JOYCE, JAMES

FINNEGANS WAKE

Atherton, J.S. "**Finnegans Wake:** 'The Gist of the Pantomime!'" **Accent** 15:14-26, Winter 1955.

— — — — —. "Lewis Carroll and **Finnegans Wake.**" **English Studies** 33:1-15, February 1952.

Beckett, Samuel.**Our Exagmination Round His Factitication for Incamation of Work in Progress.** Paris, Shakespeare and Company, Sylvie Beach, 1929.

Bernbaum, Ernest. "The Crucial Question Regarding **Finnegans**

Wake." College English 7:151-154, December 1945.

Bierman, Robert. " 'Streameress Mastress to the Sea': A Note on Finnegan's Wake." Modern Fiction Studies 2:79-80, May 1956.

Bishop, John Peale. "Finnegans Wake." Southern Review 5:439-452, Winter 1940.

Budgen, Frank. "Joyce's Chapters of Going Forth by Day." In Seon Givens, ed. James Joyce: Two Decades of Criticism. New York, Vanguard, 1948. p. 343-367. Also in Horizon 4: 172-191, September 1941.

Burgum, Edwin Berry. The Novel and the World's Dilemma. New York, Oxford University Press, 1947. p. 109-119.

Campbell, Joseph. "Finnegan the Wake." In Seon Givens ed. James Joyce: Two Decades of Criticism. New York, Vanguard, 1948. p. 368-389.

— — — — —. A Skeleton Key to Finnegans Wake. New York, Harcourt, 1944.

Chase, Richard V. "Finnegan's Wake: An Anthropological Study." American Scholar 13:418-426, Autumn 1944.

Connonlly, Cyril. The Condemned Playground; Essays: 1927-1944. New York, Macmillan, 1946. p. 1-15.

Daiches, David. The Novel and the Modern World. Chicago, University of Chicago Press, 1939. p. 147-157.

Dolmatch, Theodore B. "Notes and Queries Concerning the Revisions in Finnegans Wake." Modern Language Notes 16:142-148, June 1955.

Edel, Leon. "James Joyce and His New Work." University of Toronto Quarterly 9:68-81, October 1939.

Friedman, Melvin. Stream of Consciousness, a Study in Literary Method. New Haven, Yale University Press, 1955. p. 239-243.

Twentieth Century Criticisms

Frye, Northrop. "Blake and Joyce." **The Joyce Review** 1:39-46, February 1957.

— — — — —. "Quest and Cycle in **Finnegan's Wake**." **James Joyce Review** 1:39-47, February 2, 1957.

Glasheen Adaline. **A Census of "Finnegan's Wake;" An Index of the Characters and Their Roles.** Evanston, Northwestern University Press, 1956.

— — — — —. "**Finnegans Wake** and the girls from Boston, Mass." **Hudson Review** 7:89-96, Spring 1954.

Glendinning, A. "Commentary: **Finnegan's Wake**." **Nineteenth Century and After** 126:73-82, July 1939.

Halper, Nathan. "James Joyce and the Russian General." **Partisan Review** 18:424-431, July-August, 1951.

Higginson, Fred H. "Notes on the Text of **Finnegan's Wake**." **The Journal of English and Germanic Philology** 55:451-456, July 1956.

Highet, Gilbert. "The Revolution of the Word." **New Oxford Outlook** 1:288-304, February 1934.

Hill, Archibald A. "A Philologist Looks at **Finnegan's Wake**." **Virginia Quarterly Review** 15:650-656, October 1939.

Hodgart, M.J.C. "The Earliest Sections of **Finnegan's Wake**." **The Joyce Review** 1:3-18, February 1957.

Hodgart, M.J.C. "Shakespeare and **Finnegans Wake**." **Cambridge Journal** 6:735-752, September 1953.

Hoffman, Frederick John. **Freudianism and the Literary Mind.** Baton Rouge, Louisiana State University Press, 1945. p. 138-144.

— — — — —. "Infroyce." In Seon Givens ed. **James Joyce: Two**

Decades of Criticism. New York, Vanguard, 1948. p. 422-430.

Howarth, Robert Guy. **Literary Particles.** Sydney, Angus and Robertson, 1946. p. 42-55.

Hutchins, Patricia. **James Joyce's World.** London, Methuen, 1957. p. 214-232.

Jones, William Powell. **James Joyce and the Common Reader.** Norman, University of Oklahoma Press, 1955. p. 148-158.

Kumar, Shiv K. "Space-Time Polarity in **Finnegan's Wake.**" **Modern Philology** 54:230-233, May 1957.

Levin, Harry. **James Joyce, a Critical Introduction.** Norfolk, New Directions, 1941. p. 139-222.

Litz, Walton. "The Evolution of Joyce's **Anna Livia Plurabelle.**" **Philological Quarterly** 36:36-48, January 1957.

Magalaner, Marvin. "James Joyce and the Myth of Man." **Arizona Quarterly** 4:300-309, Winter 1948.

— — — — —. "The Myth of Man: Joyce's **Finnegan's Wake.**" **University of Kansas City Review** 16:265-277, Summer 1950.

Magalaner, Marvin and Richard M. Karn. **Joyce, the Man, the Work, the Reputation.** New York, New York University Press, 1956. p. 216-255.

Montgomery, Niall. "The Pervigilium Phoenicis." **New Mexico Quarterly** 23:437-472, Winter 1953.

Morse, J. Mitchell. "Cain, Abel, and Joyce." **ELH** 22:48-60, March 1955.

— — — — —. "Jacob and Esau in **Finnegan's Wake.**" **Modern Philology** 52:123-130, November 1954.

Peery, William. "Shakhisbeard at **Finnegan's Wake.**" **University of Texas Studies in English** 30:243-257, 1951.

Twentieth Century Criticisms

Peter, John. "Joyce and the Novel." **Kenyon Review** 18:619-632, Autumn 1956.

Ransom, John Crowe. "The Aesthetic of **Finnegan's Wake.**" **Kenyon Review** 1:424-428, Autumn 1939.

Reed, Henry. "Joyce's Progress." **Orion** 4:131-146, Autumn 1947.

Savage, Derek S. **The Withered Branch; Six Studies in the Modern Novel.** London, Eyre & Spottiswoode, 1950. p. 191-199.

Semmler, Clement. "Some Notes on the Themes and Language of **Finnegan's Wake.**" **Southerly** 15:156-171, 1954.

Smidt, Kristian. **James Joyce and the Cultic Use of Fiction.** Oslo, Okademisk Forlag, 1955. p. 68-79.

Stewart, Douglas Alexander. **The Flesh and the Spirit, an Outlook on Literature.** Sydney, Angus and Robertson, 1948. p.39-44.

Stoll, Elmer Edgar. **From Shakespeare to Joyce.** Garden City, N.Y., Doubleday, Doran, 1944. p. 350-388.

Strong, Leonard Alfred George. **The Sacred River; an Approach to James Joyce.** London, Methuen, 1949. p. 138-151.

Thompson, Francis J. "A Portrait of the Artist Asleep." **Western Review** 14:245-253, Summer 1950.

Thompson, John Hinsdale. "**Finnegan's Wake.**" In Kimon Friar and John Brinnin, eds. **Modern Poetry; British and American.** New York, Appleton-Century-Crofts, 1951. p. 505-519.

Tindall, William York. **James Joyce, His Way of Interpreting the Modern World.** New York, Scribner, 1950. p. 51-94.

Troy, William. "Notes on **Finnegan's Wake.**" In Seon Givens ed. **James Joyce: Two Decades of Criticism.** New York, Vanguard 1948. p. 302-318.

Von Phul, Ruth. "Who Sleeps at Finnegan's Wake?" **James Joyce Review** 1:27-38, June 16, 1957.

Wilson, Edmund. "The Dream of H.C. Earwicker." In his **The Wound and the Bow**. New York, Oxford University Press, 1947. p. 243-271. Also in Seon Givens ed. **James Joyce: Two Decades of Criticism**. New York, Vanguard, 1948. p. 319-342. And in John W. Aldridge. **Critiques and Essays on Modern Fiction, 1920-1951**. New York, Ronald Press, 1952. p. 160-175. And in **New Republic** 99:203-206, 270-274, June 28, July 12, 1939.

— — — — —. **Axel's Castle; a Study in the Imaginative Literature of 1870-1930**. New York, Scribner, 1939. p. 225-236.

Worthington, Mabel P. "American Folk Songs in Joyce's **Finnegan's Wake**." **American Literature** 20:197-210, May 1956.

PORTRAIT OF THE ARTIST AS A YOUNG MAN

NOTE: Criticism of the Stephen Hero published fragment is entered under this title.

Anderson, C.G. "The Sacrificial Butter." **Accent** 12:3-13, Winter 1952.

Baker, James R. "James Joyce: Esthetic Freedom and Dramatic Art." **Western Humanities Review** 5:29-40, Winter 1950-51.

Connolly, Thomas E. "Joyce's Aesthetic Theory." **University of Kansas City Review** 23:47-50, Autumn 1956.

Daiches, David. **The Novel and the Modern World**. Chicago, University of Chicago Press, 1939. p. 101-109.

Ellmann, Richard. "A Portrait of the Artist as Friend." **Kenyon Review** 18:53-67, Winter 1956.

Farrell, James T. "Joyce's **A Portrait of the Artist as a Young Man**." In Seon Givens ed. **James Joyce: Two Decades of**

Twentieth Century Criticisms

Criticism. New York, Vanguard, 1948. p. 175-197.

— — — — —. The League of Frightened Philistines. New York, Vanguard Press, 1945. p. 45-59.

Feehan, Joseph, ed. Dedalus on Crete; Essays on the Implications of Joyce's Portrait. Los Angeles, Immaculate Heart College, 1957.

Friedman, Melvin. Stream of Consciousness; a Study in Literary Method. New Haven, Yale University Press, 1955. p. 214-220.

Golding, Louis. James Joyce. London, Butterworth, 1933. p.34-68.

Gorden, Caroline. How to Read a Novel. New York, Viking, 1957. p. 210-214.

— — — — —. "Some Readings and Misreadings." Sewanee Review 61:388-393, July-September 1953.

Hackett, Francis. Horizons; a Book of Criticism. New York, Huebsch, 1919. p. 163-168.

Hendry, Irene. "Joyce's Epiphanies." In John W. Aldridge Critiques and Essays on Modern Fiction, 1920-1951. New York, Ronald Press, 1952. p. 129-142. Also in Sewanee Review 54: 449-467, Summer 1946.

Jack, Jane H. "Art and The Portrait of the Artist." Essays in Criticism 5:354-364, October 1955.

Jones, William Powell. James Joyce and the Common Reader. Norman, University of Oklahoma Press, 1955. p. 24-38.

Kenner, Hugh. "The Portrait in Perspective." In Seon Givens ed. James Joyce: Two Decades of Criticism. New York, Vanguard, 1948. p. 132-174. Also in Kenyon Review 10:361-381, Summer 1948.

The English Novel

Levin, Harry. **James Joyce, a Critical Introduction.** Norfolk, New Directions, 1941. p. 41-62.

Magalaner, Marvin and Richard M. Karn. **Joyce, the Man, the Work, the Reputation.** New York, New York University Press, 1956. p. 102-129.

Morse, J. Mitchell. "Augustine's Theodicy and Joyce's Aesthetics." **ELH** 24:30-43, March 1957.

Prescott, Joseph. "James Joyce's **Stephen Hero.**" **Journal of English and Germanic Philology** 53:214-223, April 1954.

Savage, Derek S. **The Withered Branch; Six Studies in the Modern Novel.** London, Eyre & Spottiswoode, 1950. p. 160-168.

Schorer, Mark. "Technique as Discovery." In John W. Aldridge. **Critiques and Essays on Modern Fiction, 1920-1951.** New York, Ronald Press, 1952. p. 75-77.

Seward, Barbara. "The Artist and the Rose." **University of Toronto Quarterly** 26:180-190, January 1957.

Smidt, Kristian. **James Joyce and the Cultic Use of Fiction.** Oslo, Okademisk Forlag, 1955. p. 1-67.

Spencer, Theodore. "**Stephen Hero:** The Unpublished Manuscript of James Joyce's **Portrait of the Artist as a Young Man.**" **Southern Review** 7:174-186, Summer 1941.

Tindall, William York. **James Joyce, His Way of Interpreting the Modern World.** New York, Scribner, 1950. p. 5-32.

— — — — —. **The Literary Symbol.** New York, Columbia University Press, 1955. p. 77-86.

Van Ghent, Dorothy. **The English Novel.** New York, Rinehart, 1953. p. 263-276.

Twentieth Century Criticisms

Waith, Eugene M. "The Calling of Stephen Dedalus." **College English** 18:256-261, February 1957.

Whalley, George. **Poetic Process.** London, Routledge and Kegan Paul, 1953. p. 16-24.

ULYSSES

Allen, Walter Ernest. **The English Novel; a Short Critical History.** London, Phoenix House, 1954. p. 338-342.

Beach, Joseph Warren. **The Twentieth Century Novel; Studies in Technique.** New York, The Century Co., 1932. p. 403-424.

Beach, Sylvia. **Ulysses in Paris.** New York, Harcourt Brace. 1956.

Beebe, Maurice. "James Joyce: Barnacle Goose and Lapwing." **PMLA** 71:302-320, June 1956.

Bennett, Arnold. "James Joyce's **Ulysses.**" In his **Things That Have Interested Me.** New York, Doran, 1936. p. 185-194.

Blackmur, R.P. "The Jew in Search of a Son." **Virginia Quarterly Review** 24:96-116, Winter 1948.

Brewster, Dorothy. **Modern Fiction.** New York, Columbia University Press, 1934. p. 155-217.

Brock, Hermann. "Joyce and the Present Age." **A James Joyce Year Book** 1949. p. 68-108.

Brown, Alec. "Joyce's **Ulysses** and the Novel." **Dublin Magazine** 9:41-50, January-March 1934.

Budgen, Frank Spencer Curtis. **James Joyce and the Making of "Ulysses."** New York, Smith and Haas, 1934.

Burgum, Edwin Berry. **The Novel and the World's Dilemma.** New York, Oxford University Press, 1947. p. 95-108.

Burgum, Edwin Berry. "**Ulysses** and the Impasse of Individualism." **Virginia Quarterly Review** 17:561-573, Autumn 1941.

Daiches, David. **New Literary Values.** Edinburgh, Oliver and Boyd, 1936. p. 69-82.

— — — — —. **The Novel and the Modern World.** Chicago, University of Chicago Press, 1939. p. 110-147.

Damon, S. Foster. "The Odyssey in Dublin." In Seon Givens ed. **James Joyce: Two Decades of Criticism.** New York, Vanguard, 1948. p. 203-242.

Duff, Charles. **James Joyce and the Plain Reader, an Essay.** London, Harmsworth, 1932. p. 33-62.

Duncan, Edward. "Unsubstantial Father: a Study of the Hamlet Symbolism in Joyce's **Ulysses.**" **University of Toronto Quarterly** 19:126-140, January 1950.

Duncan, Joseph E. "The Modality of the Audible in Joyce's **Ulysses.**" PMLA 72:286-295, March 1957.

Edel, Leon Joseph. **The Psychological Novel, 1900-1950.** Philadelphia, J.B. Lippincott, 1955. p. 115-139.

Edgar, Pelham. **The Art of the Novel from 1700 to the Present Time.** New York, Macmillan, 1933. p. 306-319.

Edwards, Calvin R. "The Hamlet Motif in Joyce's **Ulysses.**" **The Western Review** 15:5-13, Autumn 1950.

Edwards, Philip. "**Ulysses** and the Legends." **Essays in Criticism** 5:118-128, April 1955.

Eliot, T.S. **Ulysses** Order and Myth." In Seon Givens, ed. **James Joyce: Two Decades of Criticism.** New York, Vanguard, 1948. p. 198-202.

Ellmann, Richard. "The Background of **Ulysses.**" **Kenyon**

Twentieth Century Criticisms

Review 16:337-386, Summer 1954.

Ellmann, Richard. "The Limits of Joyce's Naturalism." **Sewanee Review** 63:567-575, Autumn 1955.

— — — — —. "Ulysses the Divine Nobody." **The Yale Review** 47:56-71, September, 1957.

Empsen, William. "The Theme of **Ulysses**." **Kenyon Review** 18:26-52, Winter 1956.

Friedman, Melvin. **Stream of Consciousness; a Study in Literary Method.** New Haven, Yale University Press, 1955. p. 220-239.

Gilbert, Stuart. **James Joyce's "Ulysses," a Study.** London, Faber, 1952.

Glasheen, Adaline. "Another Face for Proteus." **James Joyce Review** 1:3-8, June 16, 1957.

Godwin, Murray. "A Rushlight for the Labyrinth." **Pacific Spectator** 6:84-96, Winter 1952.

— — — — —. "Three Wrong Turns in **Ulysses**." **Western Review** 15:221-225, Spring 1951.

Goldberg, S.L. "Art and Freedom: the Aesthetic of **Ulysses**." **ELH** 24:44-64, March 1957.

— — — — —. "The Conception of History in Joyce's **Ulysses**." **Present Opinion** 2:62-65, 1947.

Golding, Louis. **James Joyce.** London, Butterworth, 1933. p. 89-141.

Greenway, John. "A Guide Through James Joyce's **Ulysses**." **College English** 17:67-78, November 1955.

Higgins, Bertram. "The Natural Pander: Leopold Bloom and the Others." **Calendar of Modern Letters.** 1:139-146, April 1925.

Hoffman, Frederick John. **Freudianism and the Literary Mind.** Baton Rouge, Louisiana State University Press, 1945. p. 131-138.

— — — — —. "Infroyce." In Seon Givens ed. **James Joyce: Two Decades of Criticism.** New York, Vanguard, 1948. p. 413-422.

Hueffer, Ford Madox. "**Ulysses** and the Handling of Indecencies." **English Review** 35:538-548, December 1922.

Humphrey, Robert. **Stream of Consciousness in the Modern Novel.** University of California Press, 1954. p. 87-99.

Jarrell, Mackie L. "Joyce's Use of Swift's Polite Conversation in the 'Circe' episode of **Ulysses.**" **PMLA** 72:545-554, June 1957.

Jones, William Powell. **James Joyce and the Common Reader.** Norman, University of Oklahoma Press, 1955. p. 39-148.

— — — — —. "The Common Reader and James Joyce's **Ulysses.**" **American Scholar** 21:161-171, Spring 1952.

Kain, Richard Morgan. **Fabulous Voyager.** Chicago, University of Chicago, 1947.

Kenner, Hugh. "Baker Street to Eccles Street: the Odyssey of a Myth." **Hudson Review** 1:481-499, Winter 1949.

— — — — —. "Joyce's **Ulysses**: Homer and Hamlet." **Essays in Criticism.** 2:85-104, January 1952.

— — — — —. "Pound on Joyce." **Shenandoah** 3:3-8, Autumn 1952.

Kettle, Arnold. **An Introduction to the English Novel.** London, Hutchinson's, 1951-53. v.2 p. 135-151.

Klein, A.M. "The Black Panther (A Study in Technique)." **Accent:** 10:139-155, Spring 1950.

Twentieth Century Criticisms

Knight, Douglas. "The Reading of **Ulysses**." **ELH** 19:64-80, March 1952.

Koch, Vivienne. "An Approach to the Homeric Content of Joyce's **Ulysses**." **Maryland Quarterly** 1:119-130, 1944.

Levin, Harry. **James Joyce, a Critical Introduction**. Norfolk, New Directions, 1941. p. 65-135. Also in Ray Benedict West ed. **Essays in Modern Literary Criticism**. New York, Rinehart, 1952. p. 501-513. And in John W. Aldridge. **Critiques and Essays on Modern Fiction, 1920-1951**. New York, Ronald Press, 1952. p. 143-159.

Lewis, Wyndham. **Time and Western Man**. New York, Harcourt, 1928. p. 75-113.

Litz, Walton. "Early Vestiges of Joyce's **Ulysses**." **PMLA** 71:51-60, March 1956.

Loehrich, Rolf Rudolf. **The Secret of "Ulysses."** McHenry, Ill. Compass Press, 1953.

MacCarthy, Sir Desmond. **Criticism**. London, Putnam, 1932. p. 296-311.

Magalaner, Marvin. "The Anti-Semitic Limerick Incidents and Joyce's 'Bloomsday'." **PMLA** 68:1219-1223, December 1953.

— — — — —. "Labrinthine Motif: James Joyce and Leo Taxil." **Modern Fiction Studies** 2:167-182, Winter 1956.

Magalaner, Marvin and Richard M. Karn. **Joyce, the Man, the Work, the Reputation**. New York, New York University Press, 1956. p. 146-215.

Mason, Ellsworth. "James Joyce: Moralist." **Twentieth Century Fiction** 1:196-206, January 1956.

Meagher, J.A. "A Dubliner Reads **Ulysses**." **Australian Quarterly**

17:74-86, June 1945.

Melchiori, Giorgio. "The Waste Land and Ulysses." English Studies 35:56-68, April 1954.

More, Paul Elmer. "James Joyce." American Review 5:129-157, May 1935.

Morse, J. Mitchell. "Augustine, Ayenbite, and Ulysses." PMLA 70:1143-1159, December 1955.

— — — — —. "Joyce and the Blind Stripling." Modern Language Notes 71:497-501, November 1956.

Muir, Edwin. Transition; Essays in Contemporary Literature. London, Leonard and Virginia Woolf, 1926. p. 19-45.

Muller, Herbert Joseph. Modern Fiction. New York, Funk & Wagnals, 1937. p. 290-305.

Peery, William. "The Hamlet of Stephen Dedalus." University of Texas Studies in English. 31:109-119, 1952.

Poss, Stanley. "Ulysses and the Comedy of the Immobilized Act." ELH 24:65-83, March 1957.

Pound, Ezra. "James Joyce and Pécuclet." Shenandoah 3:9-20, Autumn 1952.

Prescott, Joseph. "Homer's Odyssey and Joyce's Ulysses." Modern Language Quarterly, 3:427-444, September 1942.

— — — — —. "James Joyce: a Study in Words." PMLA 54:304-315, March 1939.

Pritchett, V.S. "Joyce's Ulysses." New Statesman and Nation 51:75-76, January 21, 1956.

Read, Herbert. Reason and Romanticism. Essays in Literary Criticism London, Faber, 1926. p. 207-223.

Twentieth Century Criticisms

    Rogers, Howard Emerson. "Irish Myth and the Plot of **Ulysses.**" **ELH** 15:306-327, December 1948.

    Rogers, William G., William York Tindall, and Lyman Bryson. "Joyce's **Ulysses.**" **Invitation to Learning** 2:63-70, Spring 1952.

    Savage, Derek S. **The Withered Branch; Six Studies in the Modern Novel.** London, Eyre & Spottiswoode, 1950. p. 169-191.

    Scheffrin, Gladys B. "Research for Meaning." **New Mexico Quarterly** 25:113-119, Spring 1955.

    Schutte, William M. **Joyce and Shakespeare; a Study in the Meaning of "Ulysses".** New Haven, Yale University Press, 1957.

    Smidt, Kristian. **James Joyce and the Cultic Use of Fiction.** Oslo, Akademisk Forlag, 1955. p. 80-98.

    Smith, Paul Jorden. **A Key to the "Ulysses" of James Joyce.** New York, Covici, 1934.

    Stanford, W.B. "Ulyssean Qualities in Joyce's Leopold Bloom." **Comparative Literature** 2:125-136, Spring 1953.

    — — — — —. **The Ulysses Theme: A Study in the Adaptability of a Traditional Hero.** Oxford, Basil Blackwell, 1954. p. 211-224.

    Stein, Sol. "The Aesthetics of James Joyce's **Ulysses.**" **University of Kansas City Review** 18:241-254, Summer 1952.

    Sternfeld, Frederick W. "Poetry and Music -- Joyce's **Ulysses.**" In Northrop Frye, ed. **Sound and Poetry: English Institute Essays 1956.** New York: Columbia University Press, 1957. p. 16-54.

    Thompson, Lawrence. **A Comic Principle in Sterne-Meredith-Joyce.** Oslo, British Institute, 1954. p. 22-32.

    Tindall, William York. "Dante and Mrs. Bloom." **Accent** 11: 85-92, Spring 1951.

Tindall, William York. **James Joyce, His Way of Interpreting the Modern World.** New York, Scribner, 1950. p. 33-50, 97-105.

— — — — —. **The Literary Symbol.** New York, Columbia University Press, 1955. p. 195-202.

Toynbee, Phillip. "A Study of James Joyce's **Ulysses.**" In Seon Givens, ed. **James Joyce: Two Decades of Criticism.** New York, Vanguard, 1948. p. 243-284.

van der Vat, D.G. "Paternity in **Ulysses.**" **English Studies** 19:145-158, August 1937.

Visser, G.J. "James Joyce's **Ulysses** and Anglo-Irish." **English Studies** 24:45-56, 79-90, April, June 1942.

Von Abele, Rudolph. "**Ulysses:** the Myth of Myth." **PMLA** 69: 358-364, June 1954.

Waldock, Arthur John Alfred. **James, Joyce, and Others.** London Williams & Norgate, 1937. p. 33-52.

West, Rebecca. **The Strange Necessity.** Garden City, Doubleday, 1928. p. 20-58.

Wickham, Harvey. **The Impuritans.** New York, Dial Press, 1929. p. 235-258.

Wilson, Edmund. "James Joyce." In Morton Dauwen Zabel. **Literary Opinion in America.** New York, Harper, 1951. p.183-206. Also in Edmund Wilson. **Axel's Castle; a Study in the Imaginative Literature of 1870-1930.** New York, Scribner, 1939. p. 191-225.

Worthington, Mabel P. "Irish Folksongs in Joyce's **Ulysses.**" **PMLA** 71:321-339, June 1956.

KINGSLEY, CHARLES

    ALTON LOCKE

        Baldwin, Stanley Everett. **Charles Kingsley.** Ithaca, N.Y.,

Twentieth Century Criticisms

    Cornell University Press, 1934. p. 93-113.

HEREWARD THE WAKE

    Baldwin, Stanley Everett. **Charles Kingsley.** Ithaca, N.Y., Cornell University Press, 1934. p. 164-173.

HYPATIA

    Baldwin, Stanley Everett. **Charles Kingsley.** Ithaca, N.Y., Cornell University Press, 1934. p. 126-143.

TWO YEARS AGO

    Baldwin, Stanley Everett. **Charles Kingsley.** Ithaca, N.Y., Cornell University Press, 1934. p. 114-125.

WESTWARD HO!

    Baldwin, Stanley Everett. **Charles Kingsley.** Ithaca, N.Y., Cornell University Press, 1934. p. 144-163.

YEAST

    Baldwin, Stanley Everett. **Charles Kingsley.** Ithaca, N.Y., Cornell University Press, 1934. p. 74-92.

    Williams, Stanley T. "**Yeast:** a Victorian Heresy." **North American Review** 212:697-704, November 1920.

LAWRENCE, D.H.

AARON'S ROD

    Gregory, Horace. **Pilgrim of the Apocalypse; a Critical Study of D.H. Lawrence.** London, M. Secker, 1934. p. 49-57.

    Hough, Graham. **The Dark Sun; a Study of D.H. Lawrence.** London, G. Duckworth, 1956. p. 95-103.

    Moore, Harry Thornton. **The Life and Works of D.H. Lawrence.** New York, Twayne Publishers, 1951. p. 194-198.

Potter, Stephen. **D.H. Lawrence; a First Study.** London, J. Cape, 1930. p. 71-78.

KANGAROO

Hough, Graham. **The Dark Sun; a Study of D.H. Lawrence.** London, G. Duckworth, 1956. p. 103-117.

Maud, Ralph. "The Politics in **Kangaroo.**" Southerly 17:67-71, 1956.

Moore, Harry Thornton. **The Life and Works of D.H. Lawrence.** New York, Twayne Publishers, 1951. p. 211-220.

Potter, Stephen. **D.H. Lawrence; a First Study.** London, J. Cape, 1930. p. 79-86.

LADY CHATTERLEY'S LOVER

Gregory, Horace. **Pilgrim of the Apocalypse; a Critical Study of D.H. Lawrence.** London, M. Secker, 1934. p. 73-83.

Hough, Graham. **The Dark Sun; A Study of D.H. Lawrence.** London, G. Duckworth, 1956. p. 148-166.

(Janett-Kerr, Martin, Father) Tiverton, Father William, pseud. "From the Death of the Gods." Reprinted from his **D.H. Lawrence and Human Existence.** London, Rockliff, 1951. In Frederick John Hoffman ed. **The Achievement of D.H. Lawrence.** Norman, University of Oklahoma Press, 1953. p. 189-201.

Murry, John Middleton. **D.H. Lawrence (Two Essays).** Cambridge, Eng., The Minority Press, 1930. (Minority Pamphlet no. 4) p. 9-15.

Rickword, Edgell. **Scrutinies.** Vol. II. London, Wishart, 1931. v.2 p. 125-129.

Spilka, Mark. **The Love Ethic of D.H. Lawrence.** Bloomington, Indiana University Press, 1955. p. 177-204.

Twentieth Century Criticisms

Spilka, Mark. "On **Lady Chatterley's Lover.**" Folio 20:29-38, Summer 1955.

THE LOST GIRL

Hafley, James. "**The Lost Girl** - - Lawrence Really Real." **Arizona Quarterly** 10:312-322, Winter 1954.

THE PLUMED SERPENT

Gregory, Horace. **Pilgrim of the Apocalypse; a Critical Study of D.H. Lawrence.** London, M. Secker, 1934. p. 62-71.

Hough, Graham. **The Dark Sun; a Study of D.H. Lawrence.** London, G. Duckworth, 1956. p. 118-138.

Jones, Keith. "Two Morning Stars." **Western Review** 17:15-25, Autumn 1952.

Moore, Harry Thornton. **The Life and Works of D.H. Lawrence.** New York, Twayne Publishers, 1951. p. 231-239.

Potter, Stephen. **D.H. Lawrence; a First Study.** London, J. Cape, 1930. p. 87-92.

Tindall, William York. "**The Plumed Serpent.**" Reprinted from his **D.H. Lawrence and Susan His Cow.** Columbia University Press, 1939. In Frederick John Hoffman ed. **The Achievement of D.H. Lawrence.** Norman, University of Oklahoma Press, 1953. p. 178-184.

THE RAINBOW

Gregory, Horace. **Pilgrim of the Apocalypse; a Critical Study of D.H. Lawrence.** London, M. Secker, 1934. p. 33-40.

Hough, Graham. **The Dark Sun; A Study of D.H. Lawrence.** London, G. Duckworth, 1956. p. 54-72.

Kettle, Arnold. **An Introduction to the English Novel.** London,

Hutchinson's, 1951-53. v.2 p. 111-134.

Lainoff, Seymour. "The Rainbow: the Shaping of Modern Man." **Modern Fiction Studies** 1:23-27, November 1955.

Leavis, F. **D.H. Lawrence, Novelist.** London, Chatto & Windus 1955. p. 96-145.

— — — — —. "The Novel as Dramatic Poem (VII): **The Rainbow** (I)." **Scrutiny** 18:197-210, Winter 1951/52.

— — — — —. "The Novel as Dramatic Poem (VII): **The Rainbow** (II)." **Scrutiny** 18:273-287, June 1952.

— — — — —. "The Novel as Dramatic Poem (VII): **The Rainbow** (III)." **Scrutiny** 19:15-30, October 1952.

Moore, Harry Thornton. **The Life and Works of D.H. Lawrence.** New York, Twayne Publishers, 1951. p. 136-144. Revised in Frederick John Hoffman ed. **The Achievement of D.H. Lawrence.** Norman, University of Oklahoma Press, 1953. p. 144-158.

Obler, Paul. "D.H. Lawrence's World of **The Rainbow.**" **Drew University Studies** No. 8, 1957.

Scott, Nathan A. **Rehearsals of Discomposure.** New York, King's Crown Press, 1952. p. 143-149.

Spilka, Mark. **The Love Ethic of D.H. Lawrence.** Bloomington, Indiana University Press, 1955. p. 93-120.

— — — — —. "The Shape of an Arch: A Study of Lawrence's **The Rainbow.**" **Modern Fiction Studies** 1:30-38, May 1955.

ST. MAWR

Craig, David and T.W. Thomas. "The Critical Forum: Mr. Liddell and Dr. Leavis." **Essays in Criticism** 5:64-80, January 1955.

Leavis, F.R. **D.H. Lawrence, Novelist.** London, Chatto &

Twentieth Century Criticisms

    Windus, 1955. p. 225-245.

    Leavis, F.R. "The Novel as Dramatic Poem (IV) **St. Mawr.**" **Scrutiny** 17:38-53, Spring 1950.

    Liddell, Robert. "Lawrence and Dr. Leavis: The Case of **St. Mawr.**" **Essays in Criticism** 4:321-327, July 1954.

SONS AND LOVERS

    Betsky, Seymour. "Rhythm and Theme: D.H. Lawrence's **Sons and Lovers.**" In Frederick John Hoffman, ed. **The Achievement of D.H. Lawrence.** Norman, University of Oklahoma Press, 1953. p. 131-143.

    Brewster, Dorothy. **Modern Fiction.** New York, Columbia University Press, 1934. p. 137-148.

    Gose, Elliot B., Jr. "An Expense of Spirit." **New Mexico Quarterly** 25:358-363, Winter 1955-56.

    Hough, Graham. **The Dark Sun; A Study of D.H. Lawrence.** London, G. Duckworth, 1956. p. 35-53.

    Moore, Harry Thornton. **The Life and Works of D.H. Lawrence.** New York, Twayne Publishers, 1951. p. 92-106.

    Muggeridge, Malcolm. "Lawrence's **Sons and Lovers.**" **New Statesman and Nation** 49:581-582, April 23, 1955.

    Spilka, Mark. "The Floral Pattern in **Sons and Lovers.**" **New Mexico Quarterly** 25:44-56, Spring 1955.

    —————. **The Love Ethic of D.H. Lawrence.** Bloomington, Indiana University Press, 1955. p. 39-89.

    Van Ghent, Dorothy. **The English Novel.** New York, Rinehart, 1953. p. 245-261.

    Weiss, Daniel. "Oedipus in Nottinghamshire." **Literature and Psychology** 7:33-42, August 1957.

THE WHITE PEACOCK

Hough, Graham. **The Dark Sun; A Study of D.H. Lawrence.** London, G. Duckworth, 1956. p. 23-35.

Moore, Harry Thornton. **The Life and Works of D.H. Lawrence.** New York, Twayne Publishers, 1951. p. 39-49.

WOMEN IN LOVE

Davis, Herbert. "Women in Love: a Corrected Typescript." **University of Toronto Quarterly** 27:34-53, October 1957.

Gregory, Horace. **Pilgrim of the Apocalypse; a Critical Study of D.H. Lawrence.** London, M. Secker, 1934. p. 40-47.

Hough, Graham. **The Dark Sun; a Study of D.H. Lawrence.** London, G. Duckworth, 1956. p. 72-90.

Leavis, F.R. **D.H. Lawrence, Novelist.** London, Chatto & Windus, 1955. p. 146-196.

— — — — —. "The Novel as Dramatic Poem (V): **Women in Love. (I)**" **Scrutiny** 17:203-220, Autumn 1950.

— — — — —. "The Novel as Dramatic Poem (V): **Women in Love (II).**" **Scrutiny** 17:318-330, March 1951.

— — — — —. "The Novel as Dramatic Poem (VI): **Women in Love (III).**" **Scrutiny** 18:18-31, June 1951.

Moore, Harry Thornton. **The Life and Works of D.H. Lawrence.** New York, Twayne Publishers, 1951. p. 157-167.

Schorer, Mark. "**Women in Love.**" In Frederick John Hoffman ed. **The Achievement of D.H. Lawrence.** Norman, University of Oklahoma Press, 1953. p. 163-177. Also in **Hudson Review** 6:34-47, Spring 1953.

Spilka, Mark. **The Love Ethic of D.H. Lawrence.** Bloomington,

Twentieth Century Criticisms

Indiana University Press, 1955. p. 121-147.

Spilka, Mark. "Star-Equilibrium in Women in Love." **College English** 17:79-83, November 1955.

LEWIS, MATTHEW

THE MONK

Varma, Devendra P. **The Gothic Flame.** London, Arthur Barker, 1957. p. 140-154.

LEWIS, WYNDHAM

THE APES OF GOD

Armstrong, Terrence Ian Fytton. **Apes, Japes, and Hitlerism. a Study and Bibliography of Wyndham Lewis.** London, Unicorn Press, 1932. p. 62-70.

Henderson, Philip. **The Novel Today; Studies in Contemporary Attitudes.** London, Lane, 1936. p. 97-102.

Wagner, Geoffrey Atheling. **Wyndham Lewis; A Portrait of the Artist as Enemy.** London, Routledge & K. Paul, 1957. p. 246-254.

THE CHILDERMASS

Wagner, Geoffrey Atheling. **Wyndham Lewis; A Portrait of the Artist as Enemy.** London, Routledge & K. Paul, 1957. p. 290-306.

THE HUMAN AGE

Kenner, Hugh. "The Devil and Mr. Lewis." **Shenandoah** 8: 15-30, Autumn 1955.

THE REVENGE FOR LOVE

Kenner, Hugh. **Wyndham Lewis.** London, Methuen, 1954. p. 123-137.

Wagner, Geoffrey Atheling. **Wyndham Lewis; A Portrait of the Artist as Enemy.** London, Routledge & K. Paul, 1957. p. 258-263.

SELF-CONDEMNED

> Wagner, Geoffrey Atheling. **Wyndham Lewis; A Portrait of the Artist as Enemy.** London, Routledge & K. Paul, 1957. p. 264-267.

SNOOTY BARONET

> Kenner, Hugh. **Wyndham Lewis.** London, Methuen, 1954. p. 107-113.

> Wagner, Geoffrey Atheling. **Wyndham Lewis; A Portrait of the Artist as Enemy.** London, Routledge & K. Paul, 1957. p. 254-257.

TARR

> Ellis, Geoffrey Uther. **Twilight on Parnassus, a Survey of Post-War Fiction and Pre-War Criticism.** London, M. Joseph, 1939. p. 360-367.

> Kenner, Hugh. **Wyndham Lewis.** London, Methuen, 1954. p. 30-49.

> Pritchett, Victor Sawdon. **Books in General.** London, Chatto, 1953. p. 248-253.

> Wagner, Geoffrey Atheling. **Wyndham Lewis; A Portrait of the Artist as Enemy.** London, Routledge & K. Paul, 1957. p. 234-244.

MATURIN, C.R.

MELMOTH THE WANDERER

> Hammond, Muriel E. "C.R. Maturin and **Melmoth the Wanderer.**" **English** 11:97-101, Autumn 1956.

> Varma, Devendra P. **The Gothic Flame.** London, Arthur Barker, 1957. p. 163-172.

LYLY, JOHN

EUPHUES

> Barish, Jonas A. "The Prose Style of John Lyly." **ELH**

Twentieth Century Criticisms

23:14-27, March 1956.

Macaulay, Rose. "Lyly and Sidney." In Derek Verschoyle, ed. **The English Novelists; a Survey of the Novel by Twenty Contemporary Novelists.** London, Chatto, 1936. p. 31-42.

Swart, J. "Lyly and Pettie." **English Studies** 23:9-18, February 1941.

EUPHUES AND HIS ENGLAND

King, Walter N. "John Lyly and Elizabethan Rhetoric." **Studies in Philology** 52:149-161, April 1955.

MACKENZIE, SIR COMPTON

THE FOUR WINDS OF LOVE

Robertson, Leo. **Compton Mackenzie; an Appraisal of His Literary Work.** London, Richards Press, 1954. p. 149-169.

GUY AND PAULINE

Robertson, Leo. **Compton Mackenzie; an Appraisal of His Literary Work.** London, Richards Press, 1954. p. 85-91.

SINISTER STREET

Robertson, Leo. **Compton Mackenzie; an Appraisal of His Literary Work.** London, Richards Press, 1954. p. 69-81.

SYLVIA SCARLETT

Robertson, Leo. **Compton Mackenzie; an Appraisal of His Literary Work.** London, Richards Press, 1954. p. 95-103.

MACKENZIE, HENRY

JULIA DE ROUBIGNE

Thompson, Harold William. **A Scottish Man of Feeling.** London, Oxford University Press, 1931. p. 145-151.

THE MAN OF FEELING

> Thompson, Harold William. **A Scottish Man of Feeling.** London, Oxford University Press, 1931. p. 107-128.

THE MAN OF THE WORLD

> Thompson, Harold William. **A Scottish Man of Feeling.** London, Oxford University Press, 1931. p. 129-138.

MAUGHAM, WILLIAM SOMERSET

CAKES AND ALE

> Cordell, Richard Albert. **W. Somerset Maugham.** New York, Nelson, 1937. p. 124-132.

OF HUMAN BONDAGE

> Brewster, Dorothy. **Modern Fiction.** New York, Columbia University Press, 1934. p. 86-94.

> Cordell, Richard Albert. **W. Somerset Maugham.** New York, Nelson, 1937. p. 88-105.

THE MOON AND SIXPENCE

> Cordell, Richard Albert. **W. Somerset Maugham.** New York, Nelson, 1937. p. 105-116.

THE RAZOR'S EDGE

> Connonlly, Cyril. **The Condemned Playground; Essays: 1927-1944.** New York, Macmillan, 1946. p. 250-254.

MEREDITH, GEORGE

THE ADVENTURES OF HARRY RICHMOND

> Beach, Joseph Warren. **The Comic Spirit in George Meredith; an Interpretation.** New York, Longmans, Green, 1911. p. 77-82.

Twentieth Century Criticisms

    Gretton, Mary (Sturge). **The Writings and Life of George Meredith; a Centenary Study.** London, Mulford, Oxford University Press, 1926. p. 100-106.

    Wright, Walter Francis. **Art and Substance in George Meredith, a Study in Narrative.** Lincoln, University of Nebraska Press, 1953. p. 94-99.

THE AMAZING MARRIAGE

    Beach, Joseph Warren. **The Comic Spirit in George Meredith; an Interpretation.** New York, Longmans, Green, 1911. p. 142-156.

    Gretton, Mary (Sturge). **The Writings and Life of George Meredith; a Centenary Study.** London, Milford, Oxford University Press, 1926. p. 216-232.

    Lindsay, Jack. **George Meredith, His Life and Work.** London, Bodley Head, 1956. p. 319-326.

BEAUCHAMP'S CAREER

    Gretton, Mary (Sturge). **The Writings and Life of George Meredith; a Centenary Study.** London, Milford, Oxford University Press, 1926. p. 113-126.

    Lindsay, Jack. **George Meredith, His Life and Work.** London, Bodley Head, 1956. p. 203-223.

    Speare, Morris Edmund. **The Political Novel.** New York, Oxford University Press, 1924. p. 237-254.

    Stevenson, Lionel. **The Ordeal of George Meredith, a Biography.** New York, Scribner, 1953. p. 198-206.

    Wright, Walter Francis. **Art and Substance in George Meredith, a Study in Narrative.** Lincoln, University of Nebraska Press, 1953. p. 102-126.

CELT AND SAXON

Hackett, Francis. **Horizons; a Book of Criticism.** New York, Huebsch, 1919. p. 65-73.

DIANA OF THE CROSSWAYS

Beach, Joseph Warren. **The Comic Spirit in George Meredith; an Interpretation.** New York, Longmans Green, 1911. p. 169-175.

Gretton, Mary (Sturge). **The Writings and Life of George Meredith; a Centenary Study.** London, Milford, Oxford University Press, 1926. p. 161-173.

Lindsay, Jack. **George Meredith, His Life and Work.** London, Bodley Head, 1956. p. 262-268.

Wright, Walter Francis. **Art and Substance in George Meredith, a Study in Narrative.** Lincoln, University of Nebraska Press, 1953. p. 140-146.

THE EGOIST

Beach, Joseph Warren. **The Comic Spirit in George Meredith; an Interpretation.** New York, Longmans, Green, 1911. p. 123-141.

Gretton, Mary (Sturge). **The Writings and Life of George Meredith; a Centenary Study.** London, Milford, Oxford University Press, 1926. p. 131-141.

Hudson, Richard B. "The Meaning of Egoism in George Meredith's **The Egoist.**" **Nineteenth-Century Fiction** 3:163-176, December 1948.

Lindsay, Jack. **George Meredith, His Life and Work.** London, Bodley Head, 1956. p. 238-244.

McCullough, Bruce Welker. **Representative English Novelists: Defoe to Conrad.** New York, Harper, 1946. p. 221-230.

Twentieth Century Criticisms

    Mayo, Robert D. "The Egoist and the Willow Pattern." **ELH** 9:71-78, March 1942.

    Stevenson, Lionel. **The Ordeal of George Meredith, a Biography.** New York, Scribner, 1953. p. 224-233.

    Van Ghent, Dorothy. **The English Novel.** New York, Rinehart, 1953. p. 183-194.

    Wright, Walter Francis. **Art and Substance in George Meredith, a Study in Narrative.** Lincoln, University of Nebraska Press, 1953. p. 60-78.

EVAN HARRINGTON

    Beach, Joseph Warren. **The Comic Spirit in George Meredith; an Interpretation.** New York, Longmans, Green, 1911. p.61-77.

    Gretton, Mary (Sturge). **The Writings and Life of George Meredith; a Centenary Study.** London, Milford, Oxford University Press, 1926. p. 44-50.

    Lindsay, Jack. **George Meredith, His Life and Work.** London, Bodley Head, 1956. p. 105-110.

LORD ORMONT AND HIS AMINTA

    Brunner, Bernard A. "Meredith's Symbolism: **Lord Ormont and His Aminta.**" **Nineteenth-Century Fiction** 8:124-133, September 1953.

    Gretton, Mary (Sturge). **The Writings and Life of George Meredith; a Centenary Study.** London, Milford, Oxford University Press, 1926. p. 207-216.

    Lindsay, Jack. **George Meredith, His Life and Work.** London, Bodley Head, 1956. p. 313-318.

ONE OF OUR CONQUERORS

    Beach, Joseph Warren. **The Comic Spirit in George Meredith;**

an Interpretation. New York, Longmans, Green, 1911. p.109-122.

Gretton, Mary (Sturge). **The Writings and Life of George Meredith; a Centenary Study.** London, Milford, Oxford University Press, 1926. p. 192-199.

Lindsay, Jack. **George Meredith, His Life and Work.** London, Bodley Head, 1956. p. 282-292.

Wright, Walter Francis. **Art and Substance in George Meredith, a Study in Narrative.** Lincoln, University of Nebraska Press, 1953. p. 186-201.

THE ORDEAL OF RICHARD FEVEREL

Beach, Joseph Warren. **The Comic Spirit in George Meredith: an Interpretation.** New York, Longmans, Green, 1911. p.34-55.

Buckler, William E. "The Artistic Unity of **Richard Feverel:** Chapter XXXIII." **Nineteenth Century Fiction** 7:119-123, September 1952.

Curtin, Frank D. "Adrian Harley: The Limits of Meredith's Comedy." **Nineteenth-Century Fiction** 7:272-282, March 1953.

Ekeberg, Gladys W. "**The Ordeal of Richard Feverel.**" **College English** 7:387-393, April 1946.

Erskine, John. **The Delight of Great Books.** Indianapolis, Bobbs-Merrill, 1928. p. 243-259.

Gretton, Mary (Sturge). **The Writings and Life of George Meredith; a Centenary Study.** London, Milford, Oxford University Press, 1926. p. 29-43.

Lindsay, Jack. **George Meredith, His Life and Work.** London, Bodley Head, 1956. p. 88-89.

Mueller, William R. "Theological Dualism and the 'System' in **Richard Feverel.**" **ELH** 18:138-154, June 1951.

Twentieth Century Criticisms

> Stevenson, Lionel. **The Ordeal of George Meredith, a Biography.** New York, Scribner, 1953. p. 60-66.
>
> Wright, Walter Francis. **Art and Substance in George Meredith, a Study in Narrative.** Lincoln, University of Nebraska Press, 1953. p. 147-161.

RHODA FLEMING

> Gretton, Mary (Sturge). **The Writings and Life of George Meredith; a Centenary Study.** London, Milford, Oxford University Press, 1926. p. 82-88.
>
> Hill, Charles J. "George Meredith's 'Plain Story'." **Nineteenth-Century Fiction** 7:90-102, September 1952.
>
> Lindsay, Jack. **George Meredith, His Life and Work.** London, Bodley Head, 1956. p. 150-157.
>
> Stevenson, Lionel. "Meredith's Atypical Novel: a Study of **Rhoda Fleming.**" University of California Publications. **English Studies** 11:89-109, 1955.
>
> Wright, Walter Francis. **Art and Substance in George Meredith, a Study in Narrative.** Lincoln, University of Nebraska Press, 1953. p. 134-139.

RICHMOND ROY

> Lindsay, Jack. **George Meredith, His Life and Work.** London, Bodley Head, 1956. p. 180-187.

SANDRA BELLONI

> Beach, Joseph Warren. **The Comic Spirit in George Meredith; an Interpretation.** New York, Longmans, Green, 1911. p. 89-107.
>
> Gretton, Mary (Sturge). **The Writings and Life of George Meredith; a Centenary Study.** London, Milford, Oxford University Press, 1926. p. 71-80.

Lindsay, Jack. **George Meredith, His Life and Work.** London, Bodley Head, 1956. p. 138-148.

Watson, Robert W. "George Meredith's **Sandra Belloni:** The "Philosopher" on the Sentimentalists." **ELH** 24:321-335, December 1957.

Wright, Walter Francis. **Art and Substance in George Meredith, a Study in Narrative.** Lincoln, University of Nebraska Press, 1953. p. 168-175.

THE SHAVING OF SHAGPAT

Lindsay, Jack. **George Meredith, His Life and Work.** London, Bodley Head, 1956. p. 63-72.

McKechnie, James. **Meredith's Allegory, "The Shaving of Shagpat."** London, Hodder and Stoughton, 1910.

Wright, Walter Francis. **Art and Substance in George Meredith; a Study in Narrative.** Lincoln, University of Nebraska Press, 1953. p. 34-42.

THE TRAGIC COMEDIANS

Beach, Joseph Warren. **The Comic Spirit in George Meredith; an Interpretation.** New York, Longmans, Green, 1911. p. 158-168.

Gretton, Mary (Sturge). **The Writings and Life of George Meredith; a Centenary Study.** London, Milford, Oxford University Press, 1926. p. 148-158.

Häusermann, Hans Walter. **The Genevese Background.** London, Routledge and Paul, 1952. p. 182-198.

Lindsay, Jack. **George Meredith, His Life and Work.** London, Bodley Head, 1956. p. 245-252.

Wright, Walter Francis. **Art and Substance in George Meredith, a Study in Narrative.** Lincoln, University of Nebraska Press, 1953. p. 175-180.

Twentieth Century Criticisms

VITTORIA

> Gretton, Mary (Sturge). **The Writings and Life of George Meredith; a Centenary Study.** London, Milford, Oxford University Press, 1926. p. 90-95.
>
> Lindsay, Jack. **George Meredith, His Life and Work.** London, Bodley Head, 1956. p. 166-177.

MOORE, GEORGE

A DRAMA IN MUSLIN

> Nejdefors-Frisk, Sonja. **George Moore's Naturalistic Prose.** Cambridge, Harvard University Press, 1952. p. 86-108.

ESTHER WATERS

> McCullough, Bruce Welker. **Representative English Novelists: Defoe to Conrad.** New York, Harper, 1946. p. 266-273.
>
> Nejdefors-Frisk, Sonja. **George Moore's Naturalistic Prose.** Cambridge, Harvard University Press, 1952. p. 109-129.

A MODERN LOVER

> Chaikin, Milton. "The Composition of George Moore's **A Modern Lover.**" **Comparative Literature** 7:259-264, Summer 1955.
>
> Nejdefors-Frisk, Sonja. **George Moore's Naturalistic Prose.** Cambridge, Harvard University Press, 1952. p. 38-56.

A MUMMER'S WIFE

> Nejdefors-Frisk, Sonja. **George Moore's Naturalistic Prose.** Cambridge, Harvard University Press, 1952. p. 57-86.

ORWELL, GEORGE

ANIMAL FARM

> Atkins, John Alfred. **George Orwell; a Literary Study.** London,

J. Calder, 1954. p. 221-232.

Brander, Laurence Robert Mean. **George Orwell.** London, Longmans, Green, 1954. p. 170-182.

BURMESE DAYS

Brander, Laurence Robert Mean. **George Orwell.** London, Longmans, Green, 1954. p. 75-91.

A CLERGYMAN'S DAUGHTER

Brander, Laurence Robert Mean. **George Orwell.** London, Longmans, Green, 1954. p. 93-100.

COMING UP FOR AIR

Brander, Laurence Robert Mean. **George Orwell.** London, Longmans, Green, 1954. p. 150-169.

KEEP THE ASPIDISTRA FLYING

Brander, Laurence Robert Mean. **George Orwell.** London, Longmans, Green, 1954. p. 101-110.

NINETEEN EIGHTY-FOUR

Atkins, John Alfred. **George Orwell; a Literary Study.** London, J. Calder, 1954. p. 237-254.

Brander, Laurence Robert Mean. **George Orwell.** London, Longmans, Green, 1954. p. 183-204.

Gleckner, Robert F. "1984 or 1948?" **College English** 18:95-99, November 1956.

Howe, Irving. "Orwell: History as Nightmare." **The American Scholar** 25:193-207, Spring 1956.

Spender, Stephen. **The Creative Element.** London, H. Hamilton, 1953. p. 128-139.

Twentieth Century Criticisms

    Voorhees, Richard J., "**Nineteen Eighty-Four:** No Failure of Nerve." **College English** 18:101-102, November 1956.

    Wadsworth, Frank W. "Orwell's Later Work." **University of Kansas City Review** 22:285-290, June 1956.

    Willison, Ian. "Orwell's Bad Good Books." **Twentieth Century** 157:354-366, April 1955.

    Woodcock, George. "Utopias in Negative." **The Sewanee Review** 64:81-97, Winter 1956.

PEACOCK, THOMAS LOVE

HEADLONG HALL

    Freeman, Alexander Martin. **Thomas Love Peacock, a Critical Study.** New York, M. Kennerley, 1911. p. 226-236.

MELINCOURT

    Freeman, Alexander Martin. **Thomas Love Peacock, a Critical Study.** New York, M. Kennerley, 1911. p. 243-253.

THE MISFORTUNES OF ELFIN

    Priestley, John Boynton. **The English Comic Characters.** London, J. Lane, 1928. p. 178-197.

    — — — — —. **Thomas Love Peacock.** New York, Macmillan, 1927. p. 177-194.

POWYS, JOHN COWPER

A GLASTONBURY ROMANCE

    Brooke, Jocelyn. "On Re-reading **A Glastonbury Romance.**" **London Magazine** 3:44-51, April 1956.

RADCLIFFE, ANN

THE MYSTERIES OF UDOLPHO

McCullough, Bruce Welker. **Representative English Novelists: Defoe to Conrad.** New York, Harper, 1946. p. 91-96.

Sypher, Wylie. "Social Ambiguity in a Gothic Novel." **Partisan Review** 12:50-60, Winter 1945.

READE, CHARLES

CHRISTIE JOHNSTONE

Burns, Wayne. "Pre-Raphaelitism in Charles Reade's Early Fiction." **PMLA** 60:1149-1164, December 1945.

THE CLOISTER AND THE HEARTH

Burns, Wayne. "**The Cloister and the Hearth:** a Classic Reconsidered." **Nineteenth-Century Fiction** 2:71-81, September 1947.

Turner, Albert Morton. **The Making of the "The Cloister and the Hearth."** Chicago, University of Chicago Press, 1938.

HARD CASH

Bowers, R.H. "The Cancelled 'Song of Solomon' Passage in Reade's **Hard Cash.**" **Nineteenth Century Fiction** 6:225-233, March 1952.

IT IS NEVER TOO LATE TO MEND

Woodring, Carl R. "Charles Reade's Debt to William Howitt." **Nineteenth-Century Fiction** 5:39-46, June 1950.

PUT YOURSELF IN HIS PLACE

Burns, Wayne. "The Sheffield Flood: a Critical Study of Charles Reade's Fiction." **PMLA** 63:686-695, June 1948.

Twentieth Century Criticisms
RICHARDSON, DOROTHY

PILGRIMAGE

Eagleson, Harvey. "Pedestal for Statue: the Novels of Dorothy M. Richardson." **Sewanee Review** 42:42-53, January-March 1934.

POINTED ROOFS

Edel, Leon Joseph. **The Psychological Novel, 1900-1950.** Philadelphia, J.B. Lippincott, 1955. p. 101-111.

RICHARDSON, SAMUEL

CLARISSA

Boas, Frederick Samuel. **From Richardson to Pinero.** London, J. Murray, 1936. p. 20-32.

— — — — —. "Richardson's Novels and Their Influence." In English Association. **Essays and Studies.** Oxford, 1911. v.2 p. 49-58.

Dobson, Henry Austin. **Samuel Richardson.** New York, Macmillan, 1902. p. 82-105.

Downs, Brian Westerdale. **Richardson.** London, G. Routledge, 1928. p. 72-83.

Elton, Oliver. **A Survey of English Literature, 1730-1780.** London, E. Arnold, 1912. v.1 p. 170-175.

Hill, Christopher. "Clarissa Harlowe and Her Times." **Essays in Criticism** 5:315-340, October 1955.

Hopkinson, H.T. "Robert Lovelace, the Romanic Cad." **Horizon** 10:80-104, August 1944.

Hughes, Helen Sard. "Characterization in **Clarissa Harlow** sic." **Journal of English and Germanic Philology** 13:110-123, January 1914.

Kettle, Arnold. **An Introduction to the English Novel.** London, Hutchinson's, 1951-53. v.1 p. 65-71.

Krutch, Joseph Wood. **Five Masters; a Study in the Mutations of the Novel.** New York, Cape & Smith, 1930. p. 149-162.

McKillop, Alan Dugald. **The Early Masters of English Fiction.** Lawrence, University of Kansas Press, 1956. p. 64-81.

— — — — —. "Epistolary Technique in Richardson's Novels." In Richard Charles Boys. **Studies in the Literature of the Augustan Age.** Ann Arbor, Mich., Distributed for the Augustan Reprint Society by the George Wahr Publishing Co., 1952. p. 41-46. Reprinted from **Rice Institute Pamphlet** 38:41-46, April 1951.

McCullough, Bruce Welker. **Representative English Novelists; Defoe to Conrad.** New York, Harper, 1946. p. 30-41.

Pritchett, Victor Sawdon. **The Living Novel.** New York, Reynal & Hitchcock, 1947. p. 24-31.

Rabkin, Norman. "**Clarissa:** A Study in the Nature of Convention." ELH 23:204-217, September 1956.

Sale, William M. "From **Pamela** to **Clarissa.**" in **The Age of Johnson: Essays Presented to Chauncey Brewster Tinker.** New Haven, Yale University Press, 1949. p. 127-138.

Thomson, Clara Linklater. **Samuel Richardson; a Biographical and Critical Study.** London, H. Marshall, 1900. p. 172-208.

Van Ghent, Dorothy. "Clarissa and Emma as Phèdre." **Partisan Review** 17:820-833, November-December 1950.

— — — —. **The English Novel.** New York, Rinehart, 1953. p.45-63.

Watt, Ian. **The Rise of the Novel; Studies in Defoe, Richardson and Fielding.** London, Chatto and Windus, 1957. p. 208-238.

Twentieth Century Criticisms

PAMELA

    Boas, Frederick Samuel. "Richardson's Novels and Their Influence." In English Association. **Essays and Studies.** Oxford, 1911. v.2 p. 41-49.

    Dobson, Henry Austin. **Samuel Richardson.** New York, Macmillan, 1902. p. 26-50.

    Krutch, Joseph Wood. **Five Masters; a Study in the Mutations of the Novel.** New York, Cape & Smith, 1930. p. 125-135.

    Lesser, Simon O. "A Note on **Pamela.**" **College English** 14: 13-17. October 1952.

    McKillop, Alan Dugald. **The Early Masters of English Fiction.** Lawrence, University of Kansas Press, 1956. p. 55-63.

    ———————. "Epistolary Technique in Richardson's Novels." In Richard Charles Boys. **Studies in the Literature of the Augustan Age.** Ann Arbor, Mich., Distributed for the Augustan Reprint Society by the George Wahr Publishing Co., 1952. p. 36-41. Reprinted from **Rice Institute Pamphlet** 38:36-41, April 1951.

    Reid, B.L. "Justice to **Pamela.**" **Hudson Review** 9:516-533, Winter 1956-57.

    Scrutton, Mary. "Bourgeois Cinderellas." **Twentieth Century** 155:351-355, April 1954.

    Thomson, Clara Linklater. **Samuel Richardson; a Biographical and Critical Study.** London, H. Marshall, 1900. p. 147-171.

    Watt, Ian. **The Rise of the Novel; Studies in Defoe, Richardson and Fielding.** London, Chatto and Windus, 1957. p. 135-173.

SIR CHARLES GRANDISON

    Boas, Frederick Samuel. **From Richardson to Pinero.** London,

J. Murray, 1936. p. 32-40.

Boas, Frederick Samuel. "Richardson's Novels and Their Influence." In English Association. **Essays and Studies.** Oxford, 1911. v.2 p. 58-65.

Dobson, Henry Austin. "**Samuel Richardson.**" New York, Macmillan, 1902. p. 138-168.

Elton, Oliver. **A Survey of English Literature, 1730-1780.** London, E. Arnold, 1912. v.1 p. 175-180.

McKillop, Alan Dugald. **The Early Masters of English Fiction.** Lawrence, University of Kansas Press, 1956. p. 81-96.

— — — — —. "Epistolary Technique in Richardson's Novels." In Richard Charles Boys. **Studies in the Literature of the Augustan Age.** Ann Arbor, Mich., Distributed for the Augustan Reprint Society by the George Wahr Publishing Co., 1952. p.46-53. Reprinted from **Rice Institute Pamphlet** 38:45-53, April 1951.

Thomson, Clara Linklater. **Samuel Richardson; a Biographical and Critical Study.** London, H. Marshall, 1900. p. 209-241.

SCOTT, SIR WALTER

THE BRIDE OF LAMMERMOOR

Gordon, Robert C. "**The Bride of Lammermoor:** A Novel of Tory Pessimism." **Nineteenth-Century Fiction** 12:110-124, September 1957.

Owen, E. "Critics of **The Bride of Lammermoor.**" **Dalhousie Review** 18:365-371, October 1938.

Parsons, Coleman O. "The Dalrymple Legend in **The Bride of Lammermoor.**" **Review of English Studies** 19:51-58, January 1943.

Twentieth Century Criticisms

GUY MANNERING

Grabo, Carl Henry. **The Technique of the Novel.** New York, Scribner's, 1928. p. 11-18.

HEART OF MIDLOTHIAN

Edgar, Pelham. **The Art of the Novel from 1700 to the Present Time.** New York, Macmillan, 1933. p. 84-89.

Kettle, Arnold. **An Introduction to the English Novel.** London, Hutchinson's, 1951-53. v.1 p. 105-122.

Mayhead, Robin. "The Heart of Midlothian: Scott as Artist." **Essays in Criticism** 6:266-277, 1956.

Pritchett, Victor Sawdon. **The Living Novel.** New York, Reynal & Hitchcock, 1947. p. 63-68.

Van Ghent, Dorothy. **The English Novel.** New York, Rinehart, 1953. p. 113-124.

IVANHOE

Duncan, Joseph E. "The Anti-Romantic in **Ivanhoe**." **Nineteenth-Century Fiction** 9:293-300, March 1955.

OLD MORTALITY

McCullough, Bruce Welker. **Representative English Novelists: Defoe to Conrad.** New York, Harper, 1946. p. 123-130.

WAVERLEY

Daiches, David. "Scott's Achievement as a Novelist." **Nineteenth-Century Fiction** 6:90-95, September 1951.

Gordon, S. Stewart. "**Waverley** and the 'Unified Design.'" **ELH** 18:107-122, June 1951.

SHELLEY, MARY WOOLLSTONECRAFT

FRANKENSTEIN

Spark, Muriel. **Child of Light, a Reassessment of Mary Woollstonecraft Shelley.** Hadleigh, Essex, Tower Bridge Publications, 1951. p. 128-149.

THE LAST MAN

Spark, Muriel. **Child of Light, a Reassessment of Mary Woollstonecraft Shelley.** Hadleigh, Essex, Tower Bridge Publications, 1951. p. 150-165.

SIDNEY, SIR PHILIP

THE ARCADIA

Boas, Frederick Samuel. **Sir Philip Sidney.** London, Staples Press, 1955. p. 57-120.

Briggs, William Dinsmore. "Political Ideas in Sidney's **Arcadia.**" **Studies in Philology** 28:137-161, April 1931.

Duhamel, P. Albert. "Sidney's **Arcadia** and Elizabethan Rhetoric." **Studies in Philology** 45:134-150, April 1948.

Goldman, Marcus Seldon. **Sir Philip Sidney and "The Arcadia."** Urbana, Ill., University of Illinois, 1934. (University of Illinois Studies in Language and Literature v.32)p. 122-210.

Greenlaw, Edwin W. "Sidney's **Arcadia** as an example of Elizabethan Allegory." In **Anniversary Papers by Colleagues and Pupils of George Lyman Kittredge.** Boston, Ginn, 1913. p.327-337.

Harman, Edward George. **The Countesse of Pembroke's Arcadia.** London, C. Palmer, 1924.

Myrick, K.O. **Sir Philip Sidney as a Literary Craftsman.** Cam-

Twentieth Century Criticisms

> bridge, Harvard University Press, 1935. (Harvard Studies in English v.14) p. 110-297.
>
> Ribner, Irving. "Machiavelli and Sidney: **The Arcadia** of 1590." **Studies in Philology** 47:152-172, April 1950.
>
> Rowe, Kenneth Thorpe. **Romantic Love and Parental Authority in Sidney's "Arcadia".** Ann Arbour, University of Michigan Press, 1947. (University of Michigan Contributions in Modern Philology no.4).
>
> Tillyard, Eustace Mandeville Wetenhall. **The English Epic and its Background.** New York, Oxford University Press, 1954, p. 294-319.
>
> Woolf, Virginia (Stephen). **The Common Reader.** Second Series. London, L. & Virginia Woolf at the Hogarth Press, 1932. p.40-50.
>
> Zandvoort, R.W. **Sidney's "Arcadia."** Amsterdam, Swets & Zeitlinger, 1929. p. 42-199.

SINCLAIR, MAY

MARY OLIVER

> Brewster, Dorothy. **Modern Fiction.** New York, Columbia University Press, 1934. p. 129-136.

THE THREE SISTERS

> Brewster, Dorothy. **Modern Fiction.** New York, Columbia University Press, 1934. p. 122-129.

SMOLLETT, TOBIAS

ADVENTURES OF PEREGRINE PICKLE

> Kahrl, George Morrow. **Tobias Smollett, Traveler-Novelist.** Chicago, University of Chicago Press, 1945. p. 28-50.
>
> McKillop, Alan Dugald. **The Early Masters of English Fiction.**

Lawrence, University of Kansas Press, 1956. p. 157-164.

Putney, Rufus D.S. "The Plan of **Peregrine Pickle.**" PMLA 60:1051-1065, December 1945.

FERDINAND COUNT FATHOM

Kahrl, George Morrow. **Tobias Smollett, Traveler-Novelist.** Chicago, University of Chicago Press, 1945. p. 51-56.

HUMPHREY CLINKER

Kahrl, George Morrow. **Tobias Smollett, Traveler-Novelist.** Chicago, University of Chicago Press, 1945. p. 119-147.

Knapp, Lewis M. "Smollett's Self-Portrait in **The Expedition of Humphrey Clinker.**" In **The Age of Johnson: Essays Presented to Chauncey Brewster Tinker.** New Haven, Yale University Press, 1949. p. 149-158.

McKillop, Alan Dugald. **The Early Masters of English Fiction.** Lawrence, University of Kansas Press, 1956. p. 170-181.

SIR LAUNCELOT GREAVES

Kahrl, George Morrow. **Tobias Smollett, Traveler-Novelist.** Chicago, University of Chicago Press, 1945. p. 56-60.

RODERICK RANDOM

Kahrl, George Morrow. **Tobias Smollett, Traveler-Novelist.** Chicago, University of Chicago Press, 1945. p. 12-27.

McCullough, Bruce Welker. **Representative English Novelists. Defoe to Conrad.** New York, Harper, 1946. p. 61-68.

McKillop, Alan Dugald. **The Early Masters of English Fiction.** Lawrence, University of Kansas Press, 1956. p. 147-157.

Twentieth Century Criticisms

STERNE, LAWRENCE

A SENTIMENTAL JOURNEY

McKillop, Alan Dugald. **The Early Masters of English Fiction.** Lawrence, University of Kansas Press, 1956. p. 214-217.

Putney, Rufus. "The Evolution of **A Sentimental Journey.**" **Philological Quarterly** 19:349-369, October 1940.

— — — — — —. "Lawrence Sterne, Apostle of Laughter." In **The Age of Johnson: Essays Presented to Chauncey Brewster Tinker.** New Haven, Yale University Press, 1949. p.167-170.

Woolf, Virginia (Stephen). **The Common Reader.** Second Series. London, L. & Virginia Woolf at the Hogarth Press, 1932. p.78-85.

TRISTRAM SHANDY

Calder-Marshall, A. "Lawrence Sterne." In Derek Verschoyle ed. **The English Novelists; a Survey of the Novel by Twenty Contemporary Novelists.** London, Chatto, 1936. p. 83-95.

Carver, Wayne. "The Worlds of Tom and Tristram." **Western Humanities Review** 12:67-74, Winter 1958.

Cash, Arthur H. "The Lockean Psychology of **Tristram Shandy.**" **ELH** 22:125-135, June 1955.

Elton, Oliver. **A Survey of English Literature, 1730-1780.** London, E. Arnold, 1912. v.1 p. 220-230.

Harper, Kenneth. "A Russian Critic and **Tristram Shandy.**" **Modern Philology** 52:92-99, November 1954.

Holland, Norman N. "The Laughter of Lawrence Sterne." **Hudson Review** 9:422-430, Autumn 1956.

Jefferson, D.W. "**Tristram Shandy** and the Tradition of Learned Wit." **Essays in Criticism** 1:225-248, July 1951.

Lehman, B.H. "Of Time, Personality, and the Author. A Study of **Tristram Shandy**: Comedy." University of California **Publications in English** 8:233-250, 1941.

Kettle, Arnold. **An Introduction to the English Novel.** London, Hutchinson's, 1951-53, v.1 p. 81-86.

McCullough, Bruce Welker. **Representative English Novelists: Defoe to Conrad.** New York, Harper, 1946. p. 71-83.

McKillop, Alan Dugald. **The Early Masters of English Fiction.** Lawrence, University of Kansas Press, 1956. p. 185-214.

MacLean, Kenneth. "The Imagination in **Tristram Shandy.**" Explorations No. 3 p. 59-64, August 1954.

Mendilow, Adam Abraham. **Time and the Novel.** London, P. Nevill, 1952. p. 165-199.

Priestley, John Boynton. **The English Comic Characters.** London, J. Lane, 1928. p. 128-157.

Putney, Rufus D.S. "Lawrence Sterne, Apostle of Laughter." In **The Age of Johnson: Essays Presented to Chauncey Brewster Tinker.** New Haven, Yale University Press, 1949. p.161-166.

Russell, H.K. "**Tristram Shandy** and the Technique of the Novel." **Studies in Philology** 42:581-593, July 1945.

Towers, A.R. "Sterne's Cock and Bull Story." **ELH** 24:12-29, March 1957.

Traugott, John Lewis. **Tristram Shandy's World.** Berkeley, University of California Press, 1954.

Van Ghent, Dorothy. **The English Novel.** New York, Rinehart, 1953. p. 83-98.

Twentieth Century Criticisms

STEVENSON, ROBERT LOUIS

DAVID BALFOUR

Daiches, David. **Robert Louis Stevenson.** Norfolk, Conn., New Directions, 1947. p. 85-93.

KIDNAPPED

Daiches, David. **Robert Louis Stevenson.** Norfolk, Conn., New Directions, 1947. p. 51-73.

THE MASTER OF BALLANTRAE

Daiches, David. **Robert Louis Stevenson.** Norfolk, Conn., New Directions, 1947. p. 74-85.

MacNaughton, John. "The Art of Robert Louis Stevenson." **Queen's Quarterly** 8:201-210, January 1901.

ST. IVES

Daiches, David. **Robert Louis Stevenson.** Norfolk, Conn., New Directions, 1947. p. 94-98.

TREASURE ISLAND

Daiches, David. **Robert Louis Stevenson.** Norfolk, Conn., New Directions, 1947. p. 32-51.

WEIR OF HERMISTON

Daiches, David. **Robert Louis Stevenson.** Norfolk, Conn., New Directions, 1947. p. 99-140.

SWIFT, JONATHAN

GULLIVER'S TRAVELS

Bracher, Frederick. "The Maps in **Gulliver's Travels.**" **Huntington Library Quarterly** 8:59-74, November 1944.

Case, Arthur Elliot. **Four Essays on "Gulliver's Travels."** Princeton, Princeton University Press, 1945.

Clubb, Merrel D. "The Criticism of Gulliver's' Voyage to the Houyhnhnms", 1926-1914." **Stanford Studies in Language and Literature.** 1941, p. 203-232.

Churchill, R.C. **English Literature of the Eighteenth Century, With a Preface on the Relations Between Literary History and Literary Criticism.** London, University Tutorial Press, 1953. p. 53-59.

Darnall, F.M. "Old Wine in New Bottles." **South Atlantic Quarterly** 41:53-63, January 1942.

Davis, Herbert John. **The Satire of Jonathan Swift.** New York, Macmillan, 1947. p. 79-106.

Dobrin, Milton B. "Lilliput Revisited: Reynolds, Fronde, Dimensional Analysis, and Dean Swift." **Technology Review** 47:299-300, 320-326, March 1945.

Eddy, William Albert. **Gulliver's Travels, a Critical Study.** Princeton, Princeton University Press, 1923.

Ehrenpreis, Irvin. "The Origins of **Gulliver's Travels.**" **PMLA** 72:880-899, December 1957.

Elliott, Robert C. "Gulliver as Literary Artist." **ELH** 19:49-63, March 1952.

Ewald, William Bragg. **The Masks of Jonathan Swift.** Cambridge, Harvard University Press, 1954. p. 125-162.

Fink, Z.S. "Political Theory in **Gulliver's Travels.**" **ELH** 14:151-161, June 1947.

Firth, Sir Charles Harding. **Essays, Historical and Literary.** Oxford, Clarendon Press, 1938. p. 210-241.

Twentieth Century Criticisms

Firth, Sir Charles Harding. "The Political Significance of **Gulliver's Travels.**" **Proceedings of the British Academy** 9:237-259, 1919/20.

Grennan, Margaret R. "Lilliput and Leprecan: Gulliver and the Irish Tradition." **ELH** 12:188-202, September 1945.

Horrell, Joe. "What Gulliver Knew." **Sewanee Review** 51:476-504, Autumn 1943.

Jarrett, James L. "A Yahoo Versus Jonathan Swift." **Western Humanities Review** 8:195-200, Summer 1954.

Kelling, Harold D. "**Gulliver's Travels:** A Comedy of Humours." **University of Toronto Quarterly** 21:362-375, July 1952.

Kliger, Samuel. "The Unity of **Gulliver's Travels.**" **Modern Language Quarterly** 6:401-415, December 1945.

Leslie, Shane. **The Skull of Swift, an Extempore Exhumation.** Indianapolis, Bobbs-Merrill, 1928. p. 230-264.

Monk, Samuel H. "The Pride of Lemuel Gulliver." **Sewanee Review** 63:48-71, Winter 1955.

Moore, John Brooks. "The Role of Gulliver." **Modern Philology** 25:467-480, May 1928.

Moore, John Robert. "The Geography of **Gulliver's Travels.**" **Journal of English and Germanic Philology** 40:214-228, April 1941.

Murry, John Middleton. **Jonathan Swift, a Critical Biography.** London, J. Cape, 1954. p. 329-355.

Newman, Bertram. **Jonathan Swift.** London, Allen & Unwin, 1937. p. 300-319.

Quintana, Ricardo. **The Mind and Art of Jonathan Swift.** London, Methuen, 1953. p. 287-327.

Quintana, Ricardo. **Swift, an Introduction.** London, Oxford University Press, 1955. p. 142-165.

Ross, John R. "The Final Comedy of Lemuel Gulliver." **University of California Publications in English** 8:175-196, 1941.

Rossi, Mario Manlio. **Swift; or The Egoist.** New York, Dutton, 1934. p. 307-350.

Smith, Sophie Shilleto. **Dean Swift.** London, Methuen, 1910. p. 222-235.

Sutherland, John H. "A Reconsideration of Gulliver's Third Voyage." **Studies in Philology** 54:45-52, January 1957.

Taylor, William Duncan. **Jonathan Swift, a Critical Essay.** London, Davies, 1933. p. 209-233.

Wedel, T.O. "On the Philosophical Background of **Gulliver's Travels.**" **Studies in Philology** 23:434-450, October 1926.

Whibley, Charles. "**Gulliver's Travels.**" **Blackwood's Magazine** 220:549-560, October 1926.

Williams, Kathleen M. "Gulliver's Voyage to the Houyhnhnms." **ELH** 18:275-286, December, 1951.

THACKERAY, WILLIAM MAKEPEACE

AMELIA

Spilka, Mark. "A Note on Thackeray's **Amelia.**" **Nineteenth-Century Fiction** 10:202-210, December 1955.

BARRY LYNDON

Matthews, James Brander. **The Historical Novel, and Other Essays.** New York, Scribner's, 1901. p. 152-162.

Ray, Gordon N. **Thackeray: the Uses of Adversity, 1811-1846.** New York, McGraw-Hill, 1955. p. 339-347.

Twentieth Century Criticisms

    Whibley, Charles. **William Makepeace Thackeray.** New York, Dodd, 1903. p. 62-76.

HENRY ESMOND

    Brown, John Macmillan. **Esmond, a Study.** Christchurch, N.Z., 1904.

    Dodds, John Wendell. **Thackeray: a Critical Portrait.** New York, Oxford University Press, 1941. p. 160-178.

    Edgar, Pelham. **The Art of the Novel from 1700 to the Present Time.** New York, Macmillan, 1933. p. 109-116.

    Ennis, Lambert. **Thackeray: the Sentimental Cynic.** Evanston, Northwestern University Press, 1950. (Northwestern University Studies, Humanities Series No. 25) p. 176-182.

    Greig, John Young Thomson. **Thackeray; a Reconsideration.** London, Oxford University Press, 1950. p. 154-166.

    Ray, Gordon N. **Thackeray: the Age of Wisdom, 1847-1863.** New York, McGraw-Hill, 1958. p. 175-194.

    Tilford, John E. "The Love Theme of **Henry Esmond.**" PMLA 67:684-701, September 1952.

    — — — — —. "The Unsavoury Plot of **Henry Esmond.**" Nineteenth-Century Fiction 6:121-130, September 1951.

    — — — — — — —. "The Untimely Death of Rachel Esmond." **Nineteenth-Century Fiction** 12:148-153, September 1957.

    Whibley, Charles. **William Makepeace Thackeray.** New York, Dodd, 1903. p. 180-193.

THE NEWCOMES

    Dodds, John Wendell. **Thackeray: a Critical Portrait.** New York, Oxford University Press, 1941. p. 192-210.

Fraser, Russell A. "Sentimentality in Thackeray's The Newcomes." Nineteenth-Century Fiction 4:187-196, December 1949.

Ray, Gordon N. **Thackeray: the Age of Wisdom, 1847-1863.** New York, McGraw-Hill, 1958. p. 236-249.

Saintsbury, George Edward Bateman. **A Considerwtion of Thackeray.** London, Oxford University Press, 1931. p. 208-220.

Whibley, Charles. **William Makepeace Thackeray.** New York, Dodd, 1903. p. 194-216.

PENDENNIS

Dodds, John Wendell. **Thackeray: a Critical Portrait.** New York, Oxford University Press, 1941. p. 137-159.

Ennis, Lambert. **Thackeray: the Sentimental Cynic.** Evanston, Northwestern University Press, 1950. (Northwestern University Studies, Humanities Series No. 25) p. 156-162.

Greig, John Young Thomson. **Thackeray; a Reconsideration.** London, Oxford University Press, 1950. p. 118-130.

Ray, Gordon N. **Thackeray: the Age of Wisdom, 1847-1863.** New York, McGraw-Hill, 1958. p. 108-130.

Saintsbury, George Edward Bateman. **A Consideration of Thackeray.** London, Oxford University Press, 1931. p. 177-191.

Whibley, Charles. **William Makepeace Thackeray.** New York, Dodd, 1903. p. 125-154.

PHILIP

Saintsbury, George Edward Bateman. **A Consideration of Thackeray.** London, Oxford University Press, 1931. p. 236-249.

VANITY FAIR

Cecil, Lord David. **Early Victorian Novelists; Essays in Re-**

Twentieth Century Criticisms

valuation. London, Constable, 1934. p. 79-91.

Chesterton, Gilbert Keith. **A Handful of Authors.** New York, Sheed and Ward, 1953. p. 56-65.

— — — — —. "**Vanity Fair.**" In Van Wyck Brooks and Others. **A Book of Prefaces.** New York, The Limited Editions Club, 1941. p. 11-18.

Dodds, John Wendell. **Thackeray: a Critical Portrait.** New York, Oxford University Press, 1941. p. 107-136.

Ennis, Lambert. **Thackeray: the Sentimental Cynic.** Evanston, Northwestern University Press, 1950. (Northwestern University Studies, Humanities Series No. 25) p. 136-149.

Fraser, Russell A. "Pernicious Casuistry: A Study of Character in **Vanity Fair.**" **Nineteenth-Century Fiction** 12:137-147, September 1957.

Greig, John Young Thomson. **Thackeray; a Reconsideration.** London, Oxford University Press, 1950. p. 102-117.

Kettle, Arnold. **An Introduction to the English Novel.** London, Hutchinson's, 1951-53. v.1 p. 156-170.

McCullough, Bruce Welker. **Representative English Novelists: Defoe to Conrad.** New York, Harper, 1946. p. 155-168.

Ray, Gordon N. **Thackeray: the Uses of Adversity, 1811-1846.** New York, McGraw-Hill, 1955. p. 384-426.

— — — — —. "**Vanity Fair:** One Version of the Novelist's Responsibility." **Transactions of the Royal Society of Literature of the United Kingdom.** Essays by Divers Hands. N.S. 25:87-101, 1950.

Saintsbury, George Edward Bateman. **A Consideration of Thackeray.** London, Oxford University Press, 1931. p. 164-176.

Tillotson, Kathleen Mary. **Novels of the Eighteen-Forties.** Oxford, Clarendon Press, 1954. p. 224-256.

Van Ghent, Dorothy. **The English Novel.** New York, Rinehart, 1953. p. 139-152.

Whibley, Charles. **William Makepeace Thackeray.** New York, Dodd, 1903. p. 90-120.

THE VIRGINIANS

Dodds, John Wendell. **Thackeray: a Critical Portrait.** New York, Oxford University Press, 1941. p. 216-221.

Ray, Gordon N. **Thackeray: the Age of Wisdom, 1847-1863.** New York, McGraw-Hill, 1958. p. 381-386.

Saintsbury, George Edward Bateman. **A Consideration of Thackeray.** London, Oxford University Press, 1931. p. 221-235.

Whibley, Charles. **William Makepeace Thackeray.** New York, Dodd, 1903. p. 220-229.

TROLLOPE, ANTHONY

THE AMERICAN SENATOR

Stryker, David. "The Significance of Trollope's **American Senator.**" **Nineteenth-Century Fiction** 5:141-149, September 1950.

Wildman, John Hazard. "Trollope Illustrates the Distinction." **Nineteenth-Century Fiction** 4:101-110, September 1949.

CAN YOU FORGIVE HER?

Hoyt, Norris D. "**Can You Forgive Her?**: a Commentary." **Nineteenth-Century Fiction** 2:57-70, September 1947.

DR. WORTLE'S SCHOOL

Cockshut, A.O.J. **Anthony Trollope; a Critical Study.** London,

Twentieth Century Criticisms

    Collins, 1955. p. 219-225.

THE EUSTACE DIAMONDS

    Cockshut, A.O.J. **Anthony Trollope; a Critical Study.** London, Collins, 1955. p. 180-196.

    Milley, H.J.W. "The Eustace Diamonds and The Moonstone." **Studies in Philology** 36:651-663, October 1939.

AN EYE FOR AN EYE

    Cockshut, A.O.J. **Anthony Trollope; a Critical Study.** London, Collins, 1955. p. 199-202.

KEPT IN THE DARK

    Cockshut, A.O.J. **Anthony Trollope; a Critical Study.** London, Collins, 1955. p. 225-228.

MR. SCARBOROUGH'S FAMILY

    Cockshut, A.O.J. **Anthony Trollope; a Critical Study.** London, Collins, 1955. p. 229-237.

ORLEY FARM

    Adams, Robert Martin. "**Orley Farm** and Real Fiction." **Nineteenth-Century Fiction** 8:27-41, June 1953.

PHINEAS FINN

    Bloomfield, Morton W. "Trollope's Use of Canadian History in **Phineas Finn** (1867-1869)." **Nineteenth-Century Fiction** 5:67-74, June 1950.

THE WARDEN

    Houston, Maude. "Structure and Plot in **The Warden.**" **University of Texas Studies in English** 34:106-113, 1955.

    Stevenson, Lionel. "Dickens and the Origin of **The Warden.**"

Nineteenth-Century Fiction 2:83-89, September 1947.

THE WAY WE LIVE NOW

 Cockshut, A.O.J. **Anthony Trollope; a Critical Study.** London, Collins, 1955. p. 204-218.

VOYNICH, E.L.

 THE GADFLY

  Kettle, Arnold. "E.L. Voynich: a Forgotten English Novelist." **Essays in Criticism** 7:163-174, April 1957.

WALPOLE, HORACE

 THE CASTLE OF OTRANTO

  Mehrotra, Kewal Krishna. **Horace Walpole and the English Novel; a Study of the Influence of "The Castle of Otranto", 1764-1820.** Oxford, B. Blackwell, 1934.

  Varma, Devendra P. **The Gothic Flame.** London, Arthur Barker, 1957. p. 42-73.

WALPOLE, HUGH

 THE CATHEDRAL

  Bidwell, Edward J. "A Twentieth Century Trollope?" **Queen's Quarterly** 30:363-371, April 1923.

 THE WOODEN HORSE

  Ashton, Winifred. **Tradition and Hugh Walpole,** by Clemence Dane (pseud.) Garden City, N.Y., Doubleday, Doran, 1929. p.122-135.

WAUGH, EVELYN

 BRIDESHEAD REVISITED

  Spender, Stephen. **The Creative Element.** London, H. Hamilton,

Twentieth Century Criticisms

    1953. p. 168-174.

    Wilson, Edmund. **Classics and Commercials.** New York, Farrar, Straus, 1950. p. 298-302.

THE LOVED ONE

    Griffiths, Joan. "Waugh's Problem Comedies." **Accent** 9:165-170, Spring 1949.

WEBB, MARY

    PRECIOUS BANE

        Addison, Hilda. **Mary Webb.** London, C. Palmer, 1931. p. 67-95.

WELLS, HERBERT GEORGE

    MR. BRITLING SEES IT THROUGH

        Hackett, Francis. **Horizons; a Book of Criticism.** New York, Huebsch, 1919. p. 125-130.

    MARRIAGE

        Scott-James, Rolfe Arnold. **Personality in Literature, 1913-1931.** New York, Holt, 1932. p. 73-76.

    THE NEW MACHIAVELLI

        Hackett, Francis. **Horizons; a Book of Criticism.** New York, Huebsch, 1919. p. 109-117.

        Scott-James, Rolfe Arnold. **Personality in Literature, 1913-1931.** New York, Holt, 1932. p. 68-73.

        Speare, Morris Edmund. **The Political Novel.** New York, Oxford University Press, 1924. p. 268-286.

    THE RESEARCH MAGNIFICENT

        Hackett, Francis. **Horizons; a Book of Criticism.** New York, Huebsch, 1919. p. 118-124.

THE SOUL OF A BISHOP

>Hackett, Francis. **Horizons; a Book of Criticism.** New York, Huebsch, 1919. p. 131-138.

TONO-BUNGAY

>Hackett, Francis. **Horizons; a Book of Criticism.** New York, Huebsch, 1919. p. 101-108.

>Kettle, Arnold. **An Introduction to the English Novel.** London, Hutchinson's, 1951-53. v.2 p. 89-95.

>Scott-James, Rolfe Arnold. **Personality in Literature, 1913-1931.** New York, Holt, 1932. p. 60-67.

WHITE, WILLIAM HALE

>THE AUTOBIOGRAPHY OF MARK RUTHERFORD

>>Merton, E.S. "The Autobiographical Novels of Mark Rutherford." **Nineteenth-Century Fiction** 5:193-203, December 1950.

>>Stock, Irvin. **William Hale White (Mark Rutherford); a Critical Study.** London, Allen and Unwin, 1956. p. 90-109.

>CATHERINE FURGE

>>Stock, Irvin. **William Hale White (Mark Rutherford); a Critical Study.** London, Allen and Unwin, 1956. p. 175-195.

>CLARA HOPGOOD

>>Stock, Irvin. **William Hale White (Mark Rutherford); a Critical Study.** London, Allen and Unwin, 1956. p. 196-220.

>MARK RUTHERFORD'S DELIVERANCE

>>Merton, E.S. "The Autobiographical Novels of Mark Rutherford." **Nineteenth-Century Fiction** 5:203-207, December 1950.

Twentieth Century Criticisms

    Stock, Irvin. **William Hale White (Mark Rutherford); a Critical Study.** London, Allen and Unwin, 1956. p. 110-130.

REVOLUTION IN TANNER'S LANE

    Stock, Irvin. **William Hale White (Mark Rutherford); a Critical Study.** London, Allen and Unwin, 1956. p. 131-152.

WILDE, OSCAR

THE PICTURE OF DORIAN GRAY

    Roditi, Edouard. **Oscar Wilde.** Norfolk, Conn., New Directions, 1947. p. 113-124.

WOOLF, VIRGINIA

BETWEEN THE ACTS

    Allen, Walter Ernest. **Reading a Novel.** London, Phoenix House, 1949. p. 40-43.

    Beck, Warren. "For Virginia Woolf." In William Van O'Connor ed. **Forms of Modern Fiction; Essays Collected in Honor of Joseph Warren Beach.** Minneapolis, University of Minnesota Press, 1948. p. 243-253.

    Bennett, Joan Frankau. **Virginia Woolf.** Cambridge, Eng., The University Press, 1945. p. 112-131.

    Blackstone, Bernard. **Virginia Woolf.** London, Hogarth Press, 1949. p. 232-242.

    Bowen, Elizabeth. **Collected Impressions.** New York, Knopf, 1950. p. 71-75.

    Chambers, R.L. **The Novels of Virginia Woolf.** London, Oliver and Boyd, 1947. p. 46-51.

    Daiches, David. **Virginia Woolf.** Norfolk, New Directions, 1942. p. 121-129.

Graham, John. "Time in the Novels of Virginia Woolf." **University of Toronto Quarterly** 18:196-201, January 1949.

Hafley, James. **The Glass Roof: Virginia Woolf as Novelist.** Berkeley, University of California Press, 1954. (University of California Publications, English Studies No. 9) p. 146-161.

Johnstone, J.K. **The Bloomsbury Group: A Study of E.M. Forster, Lytton Strachey, Virginia Woolf and their Circle.** London, Secker & Warburg, 1954. p. 370-373.

Leavis, F.R. "After **To the Lighthouse."** **Scrutiny** 10:295-298, January 1942.

Newton, Deborah. **Virginia Woolf.** Melbourne University Press, 1946. p. 57-62.

Pippett, Aileen. **The Moth and the Star: A Biography of Virginia Woolf.** Boston, Little, Brown, 1955. p. 346-350.

Savage, Derek S. **The Withered Branch; Six Studies in the Modern Novel.** London, Eyre & Spottiswoode, 1950. p. 101-105.

Zorn, Marilyn. "The Pageant in **Between the Acts."** **Modern Fiction Studies** 2:31-35, February 1956.

JACOB'S ROOM

Beach, Joseph Warren. **The Twentieth Century Novel: Studies in Technique.** New York, Appleton-Century, 1932. p. 470-473.

Bennett, Joan. **Virginia Woolf; Her Art as a Novelist.** New York, Harcourt Brace, 1945. p. 107-110.

Blackstone, Bernard. **Virginia Woolf.** London, Hogarth Press, 1949. p. 53-68.

Carew, Dudley. "Virginia Woolf." **Living Age** 330:47-54, July 1926.

Twentieth Century Criticisms

Chambers, R.L. **The Novels of Virginia Woolf.** London, Oliver and Boyd, 1947. p. 8-11, 28-29, 85-88.

Daiches, David. **Virginia Woolf.** Norfolk, New Directions, 1942. p. 55-61.

Doner, Dean. "Virginia Woolf: The Service of Style." **Modern Fiction Studies** 2:3-6, February 1956.

Friedman, Melvin. **Stream of Consciousness: A Study in Literary Method.** New Haven, Yale University Press, 1955. p.190-193.

Grabo, Carl Henry. **The Technique of the Novel.** New York, Scribner's, 1928. p. 297-305.

Gruber, Ruth. **Virginia Woolf: A Study.** Leipzig, Tauchnitz, 1935. p. 39-43.

Hafley, James. **The Glass Roof: Virginia Woolf as Novelist.** Berkeley, University of California Press, 1954. (University of California Publications, English Studies No. 9) p. 47-60.

Holtby, Winifred. **Virginia Woolf.** London, Wishart, 1932. p.116-136.

Johnstone, John Keith. **The Bloomsbury Group; a Study of E. M. Forster, Lytton Strachey, Virginia Woolf, and Their Circle.** London, Secker & Warburg, 1954. p. 328-336.

Newton, Deborah. **Virginia Woolf.** Melbourne University Press, 1946. p. 28-31.

Pippett, Aileen. **The Moth and the Star: A Biography of Virginia Woolf.** Boston, Little, Brown, 1955. p. 145-159.

MRS. DALLOWAY

Baldanza, Frank. "Clarissa Dalloway's Party Consciousness." **Modern Fiction Studies** 2:24-30, February 1956.

Beach, Joseph Warren. **The Twentieth Century Novel: Studies in Technique.** New York, Appleton-Century, 1932. p. 428-432.

Bennett, Joan. **Virginia Woolf: Her Art as a Novelist.** New York, Harcourt Brace, 1945. p. 57-64, 113-115.

Blackstone, Bernard. **Virginia Woolf.** London, Hogarth Press, 1949. p. 71-98.

Brewster, Dorothy and Angus Burrell. **Modern Fiction.** New York, Columbia University Press, 1934. p. 227-232.

Brower, Reuben Arthur. **The Fields of Light.** New York, Oxford University Press, 1951. p. 123-137.

Burgum, Edwin Berry. **The Novel and the World's Dilemma.** New York, Oxford University Press, 1947. p. 127-129.

Chambers, R.L. **The Novels of Virginia Woolf.** London, Oliver and Boyd, 1947. p. 29-32, 89-93.

Daiches, David. "Virginia Woolf." In John W. Aldridge. **Critiques and Essays on Modern Fiction, 1920-1951.** New York, Ronald Press, 1952. p. 497-502. Also in David Daiches. **The Novel and the Modern World.** Chicago, University of Chicago Press, 1939. p. 173-182. And in David Daiches. **Virginia Woolf.** Norfolk, New Directions, 1942. p. 61-78.

Doner, Dean. "Virginia Woolf: the Service of Style." **Modern Fiction Studies** 2:1-12, February 1956.

Edel, Leon. **The Psychological Novel, 1900-1950.** New York, Lippincott, 1955. p. 195-201.

Friedman, Melvin. **Stream of Consciousness, a Study in Literary Method.** New Haven, Yale University Press, 1955. p. 193-198.

Gamble, Isabel. "The Secret Sharer in **Mrs. Dalloway.**" **Accent** 16:235-251, Autumn 1956.

Twentieth Century Criticisms

Graham, John. "Time in the Novels of Virginia Woolf." **University of Toronto Quarterly** 18:186-190, January 1949.

Gruber, Ruth. **Virginia Woolf: A Study.** Leipzig, Tauchnitz, 1935. p. 43-54, 90-94.

Hafley, James. **The Glass Roof: Virginia Woolf as Novelist.** Berkeley, University of California Press, 1954. (University of California Publications, English Studies No. 9) p. 60-76.

Holtby, Winifred. **Virginia Woolf.** London, Wishart, 1932. p. 137-160.

Humphrey, Robert. **Stream of Consciousness in the Modern Novel.** Berkeley, University of California Press, 1954. p.12-14, 31-32, 51-52, 55-56, 70-72, 99-100, 102-103.

Hungerford, Edward A. " 'My Tunnelling Process': The Method of **Mrs. Dalloway.**" **Modern Fiction Studies** 3:164-167, Summer 1957.

Johnstone, John Keith. **The Bloomsbury Group; a Study of E.M. Forster, Lytton Strachey, Virginia Woolf, and Their Circle.** London, Secker & Warburg, 1954. p. 336-346.

Newton, Deborah. **Virginia Woolf.** Melbourne University Press, 1946. p. 32-37.

Pippett, Aileen. **The Moth and the Star: A Biography of Virginia Woolf.** Boston, Little, Brown, 1955. p. 195-206.

Rantavaara, Irma. **Virginia Woolf and Bloomsbury.** Helsinki, 1953. p. 105-111.

Roberts, John Hawley. "Towards Virginia Woolf." **Virginia Quarterly Review** 10:591-595, October 1934.

Roberts, John Hawley. "Vision and Design in Virginia Woolf." **PMLA** 61:835-842, September 1946.

Savage, Derek S. **The Withered Branch; Six Studies in the Modern Novel.** London, Eyre & Spottiswoode, 1950. p. 80-87.

Steinberg, Erwin. "Freudian Symbolism and Communication." **Literature and Psychology** 3:2-4, April 1953.

Tindall, William York. **The Literary Symbol.** New York, Columbia University Press, 1955. p. 203-205.

Wright, Nathalia. "Mrs. Dalloway: A Study in Composition." **College English** 5:351-358, April 1944.

NIGHT AND DAY

Bennett, Joan. **Virginia Woolf: Her Art as a Novelist.** New York, Harcourt Brace, 1945. p. 6-15.

Blackstone, Bernard. **Virginia Woolf.** London; Hogarth Press, 1949. p. 32-46.

Daiches, David. **Virginia Woolf.** Norfolk, New Directions, 1942. p. 17-33.

Gruber, Ruth. **Virginia Woolf: A Study.** Leipzig, Tauchnitz, 1935. p. 9-16.

Hafley, James. **The Glass Roof: Virginia Woolf as Novelist.** Berkeley, University of California Press, 1954. (University of California Publications, English Studies No. 9) p. 26-39, 47-60.

Holtby, Winifred. **Virginia Woolf.** London, Wishart, 1932. p. 83-97.

Johnstone, J.K. **The Bloomsbury Group: A Study of E.M. Forster, Lytton Strachey, Virginia Woolf and Their Circle.** London, Secker & Warburg, 1954. p. 321-327.

Mais, Stuart P.B. **Why We Should Read.** New York, Dodd, Mead, 1921. p. 105-111.

Twentieth Century Criticisms

Mansfield, Katherine. **Novels and Novelists.** New York, Knopf, 1930. p. 112-115.

Newton, Deborah. **Virginia Woolf.** Melbourne University Press, 1946. p. 25-27.

Pippett, Aileen. **The Moth and the Star: A Biography of Virginia Woolf.** Boston, Little, Brown, 1955. p. 119-129.

ORLANDO

Baldanza, Frank. "**Orlando** and the Sackvilles." **PMLA** 70: 274-279, March 1955.

Blackstone, Bernard. **Virginia Woolf: A Commentary.** New York, Harcourt Brace, 1949. p. 131-138.

Daiches, David. **Virginia Woolf.** Norfolk, New Directions, 1942. p. 97-103.

Gruber, Ruth. **Virginia Woolf: A Study.** Leipzig, Tauchnitz, 1935. p. 17-23, 34-37, 85-89.

Hafley, James. **The Glass Roof: Virginia Woolf as Novelist.** Berkeley, University of California Press, 1954. (University of California Publications, English Studies No. 9) p. 92-105.

Holtby, Winifred. **Virginia Woolf.** London, Wishart, 1932. p. 161-185.

Hunting, Constance. "The Technique of Persuasion in **Orlando.**" **Modern Fiction Studies** 2:17-23, February 1956.

Lorberg, Aileen D. "Virginia Woolf, Benevolent Satirist." **The Personalist** 33:154-158, 1952.

Mendilow, A.A. **Time and the Novel.** London, Peter Nevill, 1952. p. 228-231.

Newton, Deborah. **Virginia Woolf.** Melbourne University Press, 1946. p. 41-47.

Pippett, Aileen. **The Moth and the Star: A Biography of Virginia Woolf.** Boston, Little, Brown, 1955. p. 254-272.

Rantavaara, Irma. **Virginia Woolf and Bloomsbury.** Helsinki, 1953. p. 131-138.

TO THE LIGHTHOUSE

Aiken, Conrad. "The Novel as a Work of Art." **Dial** 83:41-44, July 1927.

Auerbach, Erich. **Mimesis: The Representation of Reality in Western Literature.** Princeton, Princeton University Press, 1953. p. 525-553.

Baldanza, Frank. "**To the Lighthouse** Again." **PMLA** 70:548-552, June 1955.

Bennett, Joan. **Virginia Woolf: Her Art as a Novelist.** New York, Harcourt Brace, 1945. p. 35-38. 70-73, 115-120.

Blackstone, Bernard. **Virginia Woolf.** London, Hogarth Press, 1949. p. 99-130.

Blotner, Joseph L. "Mythic Patterns in **To the Lighthouse.**" **PMLA** 71:547-562, September 1956.

Brewster, Dorothy. **Modern Fiction.** New York, Columbia University Press, 1934. p. 236-242.

Brown, Edward Killoran. **Rhythm in the Novel.** University of Toronto Press, 1950. p. 63-70.

Burgum, Edwin Berry. **The Novel and the World's Dilemma.** New York, Oxford University Press, 1947. p. 123-124, 129-134.

Chambers, R.L. **The Novels of Virginia Woolf.** London, Oliver and Boyd, 1947. p. 32-38.

Daiches, David. **Virginia Woolf.** Norfolk, New Directions, 1942. p. 79-96.

Twentieth Century Criticisms

Derbyshire, S.H. "An Analysis of Mrs. Woolf's To the Lighthouse." College English 3:353-360, January 1942.

Edel, Leon Joseph. The Psychological Novel, 1900-1950. Philadelphia, J.B. Lippincott, 1955. p. 195-201.

Friedman, Melvin. Stream of Consciousness; a Study in Literary Method. New Haven, Yale University Press, 1955. p.198-203.

Friedman, Norman. "The Waters of Annihilation: Double Vision in To the Lighthouse." ELH 22:61-79, March 1955.

Graham, John. "Time in the Novels of Virginia Woolf." University of Toronto Quarterly 18:190-192, January 1949.

Gruber, Ruth. Virginia Woolf: A Study. Leipzig, Tauchnitz, 1935. p. 54-63.

Hafley, James. The Glass Roof: Virginia Woolf as Novelist. Berkeley, University of California Press, 1954. (University of California Publications, English Studies No. 9) p. 77-92.

Hoare, Dorothy. Some Studies in the Modern Novel. London, Chatto & Windus, 1938. p. 53-62.

Holtby, Winifred. Virginia Woolf. London, Wishart, 1932. p. 137-160.

Humphrey, Robert. Stream of Consciousness in the Modern Novel. Berkeley, University of California Press, 1954. p.100-102.

Johnstone, John Keith. The Bloomsbury Group; a Study of E.M. Forster, Lytton Strachey, Virginia Woolf, and Their Circle. London, Secker & Warburg, 1954. p. 346-356.

Kettle, Arnold. An Introduction to the English Novel. London, Hutchinson's, 1951-53. v.2 p. 100-105.

Newton, Deborah. Virginia Woolf. Melbourne University Press,

1946. p. 37-40.

Overcarsh, F.L. "The Lighthouse, Face to Face." **Accent** 10:107-123, Winter 1950.

Pippett, Aileen. **The Moth and the Star: A Biography of Virginia Woolf.** Boston, Little, Brown, 1955. p. 227-238.

Rantavaara, Irma. **Virginia Woolf and Bloomsbury.** Helsinki, 1953. p. 112-130.

Roberts, John Hawley. "Towards Virginia Woolf." **Virginia Quarterly Review** 10:595-598, October 1934.

— — — — —. "'Vision and Design' in Virginia Woolf." **PMLA** 61:842-847, September 1946.

Savage, Derek, S. **The Withered Branch; Six Studies in the Modern Novel.** London, Eyre & Spottiswoode, 1950. p. 87-94.

Tindall, William York. **The Literary Symbol.** New York, Columbia University Press, 1955. p. 158-163.

THE VOYAGE OUT

Bennett, Joan. **Virginia Woolf: Her Art as a Novelist.** New York, Harcourt Brace, 1945. p. 4-15.

Blackstone, Bernard. **Virginia Woolf.** London, Hogarth Press, 1949. p. 15-31.

Daiches, David. **Virginia Woolf.** Norfolk, New Directions, 1942. p. 9-17.

Gruber, Ruth. **Virginia Woolf: A Study.** Leipzig, Tauchnitz, 1935. p. 9-16.

Hafley, James. **The Glass Roof: Virginia Woolf as Novelist.** Berkeley, University of California Press, 1954. (University of California Publications, English Studies No. 9) p. 14-26.

Twentieth Century Criticisms

    Holtby, Winifred. **Virginia Woolf.** London, Wishart, 1932. p. 61-80.

    Johnstone, J.K. **The Bloomsbury Group: A Study of E.M. Forster, Lytton Strachey, Virginia Woolf and Their Circle.** London, Secker & Warburg, 1954. p. 126-128, 321-327.

    Newton, Deborah. **Virginia Woolf.** Melbourne University Press, 1946. p. 20-25.

    Pippett, Aileen. **The Moth and the Star: A Biography of Virginia Woolf.** Boston, Little, Brown, 1955. p. 107-119.

THE WAVES

    Bennett, Joan. **Virginia Woolf: Her Art as a Novelist.** New York, Harcourt Brace, 1945. p. 39-43, 54-57, 120-127.

    Bevis, Dorothy "**The Waves:** a Fusion of Symbol, Style and Thought in Virginia Woolf." **Twentieth Century Literature** 2:5-20, April 1956.

    Blackstone, Bernard. **Virginia Woolf.** London, Hogarth Press, 1949. p. 165-181.

    Daiches, David. **Virginia Woolf.** Norfolk, New Directions, 1942. p. 103-111.

    Dobrée, Bonamy. **Modern Prose Style.** Oxford, Clarendon, 1934. p. 51-55.

    Friedman, Melvin. **Stream of Consciousness: A Study in Literary Method.** New Haven, Yale University Press, 1955. p. 204-207.

    Graham, John. "Time in the Novels of Virginia Woolf." **University of Toronto Quarterly** 18:192-195, January 1949.

    Gruber, Ruth. **Virginia Woolf: A Study.** Leipzig, Tauchnitz, 1935. p. 64-77.

Hafley, James. **The Glass Roof: Virginia Woolf as Novelist.** Berkeley, University of California Press, 1954. (University of Califonria Publications, English Studies No. 9) p. 105-131.

Havard-Williams, Peter and Margaret Havard-Williams. "Bateau Irve: The Symbol of the Sea in Virginia Woolf's **The Waves." English Studies** 34:9-17, February 1953.

— — — — —. "Mystical Experience in Virginia Woolf's **The Waves." Essays in Criticism** 4:71-84, January 1954.

— — — — —. "Perceptive Contemplation in the Work of Virginia Woolf." **English Studies** 35:97-116, June 1954.

Holtby, Winifred. **Virginia Woolf.** London, Wishart, 1932. p.186-203.

Johnstone, John Keith. **The Bloomsbury Group; a Study of E.M. Forster, Lytton Strachey, Virginia Woolf and Their Circle.** London, Secker & Warburg, 1954. p. 357-368.

Newton, Deborah. **Virginia Woolf.** Melbourne University Press, 1946. p. 47-52.

Pippett, Aileen. **The Moth and the Star: A Biography of Virginia Woolf.** Boston, Little, Brown, 1955. p. 288-293.

Roberts, John Hawley. "Towards Virginia Woolf." **Virginia Quarterly Review** 10:598-602, October 1934.

Toynbee, Philip. "Virginia Woolf: A Study of Three Experimental Novels." **Horizon** 14:299-304, November 1946.

THE YEARS

Blackstone, Bernard. **Virginia Woolf.** London, Hogarth Press, 1949. p. 194-205.

Daiches, David. **Virginia Woolf.** Norfolk, New Directions, 1942. p. 111-121.

Twentieth Century Criticisms

Hafley, James. **The Glass Roof: Virginia Woolf as Novelist.** Berkeley, University of California Press, 1954. (University of California Publications, English Studies No. 9) p. 132-146.

Hartley, Lodwick. "Of Time and Mrs. Woolf." **Sewanee Review** 47:235-241, April-June 1939.

Mellers, W.H. "Mrs. Woolf and Life." **Scrutiny** 6:71-75, June 1937.

Newton, Deborah. **Virginia Woolf.** Melbourne University Press, 1946. p. 52-56.

Pippett, Aileen. **The Moth and the Star: A Biography of Virginia Woolf.** Boston, Little, Brown, 1955. p. 327-335.

Roberts, John Hawley. "The End of the English Novel?" **Virginia Quarterly Review** 13:437-439, Summer 1937.

Savage, D.S. **The Withered Branch: Six Studies in the Modern Novel.** London, Eyre and Spottiswoode, 1950. p. 97-101.

Van Doren, Mark. **The Private Reader.** New York, Holt, 1942. p. 262-266.

*SOURCES

* The following is not a list of sources checked but of those books and periodicals in which criticisms were found.

BOOKS

Addison, Hilda. **Mary Webb.** London, C. Palmer, 1931.

The Age of Johnson: Essays Presented to Chauncey Brewster Tinker, New Haven, Yale University Press, 1949.

Aldridge, John W. **Critiques and Essays on Modern Fiction, 1920-1951.** New York, Ronald Press, 1952.

Allen, Walter Ernest. **Arnold Bennett.** Denver, A. Swallow, 1949.

— — — — —. **The English Novel; a Short Critical History.** London, Phoenix House, 1954.

— — — — —. **Reading a Novel.** London, Phoenix House, 1949.

— — — — —. **Six Great Novelists.** London, H. Hamilton, 1955.

Allott, Kenneth and Miriam Farris (Allott). **The Art of Graham Greene.** London, Hamish Hamilton, 1951.

Anniversary Papers by Colleagues and Pupils of George Lyman Kittredge. Boston, Ginn, 1913.

Armstrong, Terrence Ian Fytton. **Apes, Japes, and Hitlerism. A Study and Bibliography of Wyndham Lewis.** London, Unicorn Press, 1932.

Ashley, Robert. **Wilkie Collins.** London, Arthur Barker, 1952.

Ashton, Winifred. **Tradition and Hugh Walpole,** by Clemence Dane (pseud.) Garden City, N.Y. Doubleday, Doran, 1929.

Atkins, John Alfred. **George Orwell; a Literary Study.** London, J. Calder, 1954.

Auerbach, Erich. **Mimesis: the Representation of Reality in Western Literature.** Princeton, Princeton University Press, 1953.

Twentieth Century Criticisms

Bailey, John Cann. **Introductions to Jane Austen.** London, Oxford University Press, 1931.

Baker, Denys Val, ed. **Writers of To-day.** London, Sidgwick, 1946.

Baker, Richard Merriam. **The Drood Murder Case; Five Studies in Dickens' Edwin Drood.** Berkeley, University of California Press, 1951.

Bald, Marjory Amelia. **Women-Writers of the Nineteenth Century.** Cambridge, England, The University Press, 1923.

Baldwin, Stanley Everett. **Charles Kingsley.** Ithaca, N.Y. Cornell University Press, 1934.

Banerji, Hiran Kumar. **Henry Fielding, Playwright, Journalist and Master of the Art of Fiction.** Oxford, Blackwell, 1929.

Beach, Joseph Warren. **The Comic Spirit in George Meredith; an Interpretation.** New York, Longmans, Green, 1911.

— — — — —. **The Technique of Thomas Hardy.** Chicago, University of Chicago Press, 1922.

— — — — —. **The Twentieth Century Novel; Studies in Technique.** New York, The Century Co., 1932.

Beach, Sylvia. **Ulysses in Paris.** New York, Harcourt Brace, 1956.

Beckett, Samuel. **Our Exagmination Round His Factification for Incamation of Work in Progress.** Paris, Shakespeare and Company, Sylvia Beach, 1929.

Bekker, William Gerard. **An Historical and Critical Review of Samuel Butler's Literary Works.** Rotterdam, Gedrukt bij Nijgh & Van Ditmar, 1925.

Bennett, Arnold. **Things That Have Interested Me.** New York, Doran, 1936.

Bennett, Joan (Frankau). **George Eliot, Her Mind and Her Art.** Cambridge, University Press, 1948.

———. **Virginia Woolf.** Cambridge, Eng., The University Press, 1945.

Bissell, Frederick Olds. **Fielding's Theory of the Novel.** Ithaaca, N.Y., Cornell University Press, 1933.

Blackstone, Bernard. **Virginia Woolf.** London, Hogarth Press, 1949.

Boas, Frederick Samuel. **From Richardson to Pinero.** London, J. Murray, 1936.

———. **Sir Philip Sidney.** London, Staples Press, 1955.

Bowen, Elizabeth. **Collected Impressions.** New York, Knopf, 1950.

Boys, Richard Charles. **Studies in the Literature of the Augustan Age.** Ann Arbor, Mich., Distributed for the Augustan Reprint Society by the George Wahr Publishing Co., 1952.

Brander, Laurence Robert Mean. **George Orwell.** London, Longmans, Green, 1954.

Braybrooke, Patrick. **Thomas Hardy and His Philosophy.** London, C.W. Daniel, 1928.

Brewster, Dorothy and Angus Burrell. **Modern Fiction.** New York, Columbia University Press, 1934.

Brittain, Vera Mary. **In the Steps of John Bunyan; an Excursion into Puritan England.** London, Rich and Cowan, 1951. (American title, **Valiant Pilgrim**).

Brower, Reuben Arthur. **The Fields of Light.** New York, Oxford University Press, 1951.

Twentieth Century Criticisms

Brooks, Van Wyck, and others. **A Book of Prefaces.** New York, The Limited Editions Club, 1941.

Brown, Douglas. **Thomas Hardy.** London, Longmans, 1954.

Brown, Edward Killoran. **Rhythm in the Novel.** University of Toronto Press, 1950.

Brown, John Macmillan. **Esmond, a Study.** Christchurch, N.Z., 1904.

Budgen, Frank Spencer Curtis. **James Joyce and the Making of "Ulysses".** New York, Smith and Haas, 1934.

Bullett, Gerald William. **George Eliot, Her Life and Books.** London, Collins, 1947.

Burgum, Edwin Berry. **The Novel and the World's Dilemma.** New York, Oxford University Press, 1947.

Butt, John and Kathleen Tillotson. **Dickens at Work.** London, Methuen, 1957.

Campbell, Joseph and Henry Morton Robinson. **A Skeleton Key to "Finnegan's Wake".** New York, Harcourt, 1944.

Cannan, Gilbert. **Samuel Butler; a Critical Study.** London, M. Secker, 1915.

Case, Arthur Elliot. **Four Essays on "Gulliver's Travels".** Princeton, Princeton University Press, 1945.

Cecil, Lord David. **Early Victorian Novelists: Essays in Revaluation.** London, Constable, 1934.

Chambers, R.L. **The Novels of Virginia Woolf.** London, Oliver and Boyd, 1947.

Chase, Mary Ellen. **Thomas Hardy from Serial to Novel.** Minneapolis, University of Minneapolis Press, 1927.

Chesterton, Gilbert Keith. **Charles Dickens.** London, Methuen, 1936.

— — — — — —. **Criticisms and Appreciations of the Works of Charles Dickens.** London, Dent, 1933.

— — — — —. **A Handful of Authors.** New York, Sheed and Ward, 1953.

Chevrillon, Andre. **Three Studies in English Literature: Kipling, Galsworthy, Shakespeare.** From the French by Florence Simmonds, New York, Doubleday, Page, 1923.

Chew, Samuel Daggett. **Thomas Hardy, Poet and Novelist.** New York, Knopf, 1929.

Churchill, R.C. **English Literature of the Eighteenth Century, With a Preface on the Relations Between Literary History and Literary Criticism.** London, University Tutorial Press, 1953.

Cockshut, A.O.J. **Anthony Trollope; a Critical Study.** London, Collins, 1955.

Cole, George Douglas Howard. **Samuel Butler and "The Way of All Flesh."** London, Home & Van Thal, 1947.

Connonlly, Cyril. **The Condemned Playground; Essays: 1927-1944.** New York, Macmillan, 1946.

Cordell, Richard Albert. **W. Somerset Maugham.** New York, Nelson, 1937.

Crane, Ronald Salmon, ed. **Critics and Criticism Ancient and Modern.** Chicago, University of Chicago Press, 1952.

Crankshaw, Edward. **Joseph Conrad; Some Aspects of the Art of the Novel.** London, John Lane, 1936.

Croman, Natalie. **John Galsworthy, a Study in Continuity and Contrast.** Cambridge, Mass., Harvard University Press, 1933.

Cross, Wilbur Lucius. **The History of Henry Fielding.** New Haven, Yale University Press, 1928.

Twentieth Century Criticisms

Daiches, David. **New Literary Values.** Edinburgh, Oliver and Boyd, 1936.

— — — — —. **The Novel and the Modern World.** Chicago, University of Chicago Press, 1939.

— — — — —. **Robert Louis Stevenson.** Norfolk, Conn., New Directions, 1947.

— — — — —. **Virginia Woolf.** Norfolk, New Directions, 1942.

Davis, Herbert John, ed. **Nineteenth-Century Studies.** Ithaca, New York, Cornell University Press, 1940.

— — — — —. **The Satire of Jonathan Swift.** New York, Macmillan, 1947.

Digeon, Aurélieu. **The Novels of Fielding.** London, Routledge, 1925.

Dobrée, Bonamy. **Modern Prose Style.** Oxford Clarendon, 1934.

— — — — —. **Variety of Ways.** Oxford, Clarendon Press, 1932.

Dobson, Henry Austin. **Fielding.** London, Macmillan, 1907.

— — — — —. **Samuel Richardson.** New York, Macmillan, 1902.

Dodds, John Wendell. **Thackeray: a Critical Portrait.** New York, Oxford University Press, 1941.

Donnelly, Mabel Collins. **George Gissing, Grave Comedian.** Cambridge, Harvard University Press, 1954.

Downs, Brian Westerdale. **Richardson.** London, G. Routledge, 1928.

Dry, Florence (Swinton). **The Sources of "Jane Eyre".** Cambridge, England, W. Heffer, 1940.

— — — — —. **The Sources of "Wuthering Heights".** Cambridge, England, W. Heffer, 1937.

Dudden, Frederick Homes. **Henry Fielding: His Life, Works, and Times.** Oxford, Clarendon Press, 1952.

Duff, Charles. **James Joyce and the Plain Reader.** London, Harmsworth, 1932.

Duffin, Henry Charles. **Thomas Hardy; a Study of the Wessex Novels.** Manchester, University Press, 1921.

Eddy, William Albert. **Gulliver's Travels, a Critical Study.** Princeton, Princeton University Press, 1923.

Edel, Leon Joseph. **The Psychological Novel, 1900-1950.** Philadelphia, J.B. Lippincott, 1955.

Edgar, Pelham. **The Art of the Novel From 1700 to the Present Time.** New York, Macmillan, 1933.

Eliot, T.S. **Selected Essays, 1917-1932.** London, Faber & Faber, 1932.

Ellis, Geoffrey Uther. **Twilight on Parnassus; a Survey of Post-War Fiction and Pre-War Criticism.** London, M. Joseph, 1939.

Elton, Oliver. **A Survey of English Literature, 1730-1780.** London, E. Arnold, 1912.

Erskine, John. **The Delight of Great Books.** Indianapolis, Bobbs-Merrill, 1928.

Ewald, William Bragg. **The Masks of Jonathan Swift.** Cambridge, Harvard University Press, 1954.

Farrell, James Thomas. **The League of Frightened Philistines.** New York, Vanguard Press, 1945.

Feehan, Joseph ed. **Dedalus on Crete; Essays on the Implication of Joyce's Portrait.** Los Angeles, Immaculate Heart College, 1957.

Twentieth Century Criticisms

Ffrench, Yvonne. **Mrs. Gaskell.** London, Home & Van Thal, 1949.

Firkins, Oscar W. **Jane Austen.** New York, Holt, 1920.

Firth, Sir Charles Harding. **Essays, Historical and Literary.** Oxford, Clarendon Press, 1938.

Fleisher, David. **William Godwin.** London, Allen & Unwin, 1951.

Follett, Wilson. **Joseph Conrad; a Short Study of His Intellectual and Emotional Attitude Toward His Work and of the Chief Characteristics of His Novels.** Garden City, New York, Doubleday, Page, 1915.

Freeman, Alexander Martin. **Thomas Love Peacock, a Critical Study.** New York, M. Kennerley, 1911.

Friar, Kimon and John Brinnin, eds. **Modern Poetry: British and American.** New York, Appleton-Century-Crofts, 1951.

Friedman, Melvin. **Stream of Consciousness; a Study in Literary Method.** New Haven, Yale University Press, 1955.

Frye, Northrop. **Sound and Poetry. English Institute Essays, 1956.** New York, Columbia University Press, 1957.

Furbank, Philip Nickolas. **Samuel Butler (1835-1902).** Cambridge, University Press, 1948.

Garnett, Martha (Roscoe). **Samuel Butler and His Family Relations.** London, Dent, 1926.

Gilbert, Stuart. **James Joyce's "Ulysses", a Study.** London, Faber, 1952.

Gissing, George Robert. **Critical Studies of the Works of Charles Dickens.** New York, Greenberg, 1924.

Givens, Seon, ed. **James Joyce: Two Decades of Criticism.**

New York, Vanguard, 1948.

Golding, Louis. **James Joyce.** London, Butterworth, 1933.

Gorden, Caroline. **How to Read a Novel.** New York, Viking,1957.

Gordon, John Dozier. **Joseph Conrad; the Making of a Novelist.** Cambridge, Mass., Harvard University Press, 1940.

Grabo, Carl Henry. **The Technique of the Novel.** New York, Scribner's, 1928.

Greene, Graham. **The Lost Childhood and Other Essays.** London, Eyre & Spottiswoode, 1951.

Gregory, Horace. **Pilgrim of the Apocalypse; a Critical Study of D.H. Lawrence.** London, M. Secker, 1934.

Greig, John Young Thomson. **Thackeray; a Reconsideration.** London, Oxford University Press, 1950.

Gretton, Mary (Sturge). **The Writings and Life of George Meredith; a Centenary Study.** London, Milford, Oxford University Press, 1926.

Griffith, Gwilyn Oswald. **John Bunyan.** London, Hodder, 1929.

Grimsditch, Herbert B. **Character and Environment in the Novels of Thomas Hardy.** London, H.F. & G. Witherby, 1925.

Gruber, Ruth. **Virginia Woolf: a Study.** Leipzig, Tauchnitz, 1935.

Guerard, Albert J. **Thomas Hardy; the Novels and the Stories.** Cambridge, Harvard University Press, 1949.

Hackett, Francis. **Horizons; a Book of Criticism.** New York, Huebsch, 1919.

Hafley, James Robert. **Virginia Woolf as a Novelist.** Berkeley, University of California Press, 1954. (University of California Publications, English Studies No. 9).

Twentieth Century Criticisms

Haldane, Elizabeth Sandison. **George Eliot and Her Times; a Victorian Study.** New York, Appleton, 1927.

Hanson, Lawrence. **Marian Evans and George Eliot.** London, Oxford University Press, 1952.

Harman, Edward George. **The Countesse of Pembroke's "Arcadia".** London, C. Palmer, 1924.

Harris, John F. **Samuel Butler.** London, G. Richards, 1916.

Haüssermann, Hans Walter. **The Genevese Background.** London, Routledge and Paul, 1952.

Henderson, Alexander. **Aldous Huxley.** New York, Harper, 1936.

Henderson, Philip. **The Novel Today; Studies in Contemporary Attitudes.** London, Lane, 1936.

Henkin, Leo Justin. **Darwinism in the English Novel, 1860-1910.** New York, Corporate Press, 1940.

Hewitt, Douglas John. **Conrad; a Reassessment.** Cambridge, Bowes & Bowes, 1952.

Hinkley, Laura L. **The Brontës, Charlotte and Emily.** New York, Hastings House, 1945.

Hoare, Dorothy. **Some Studies in the Modern Novel.** London, Chatto and Windus, 1938.

Hoffman, Frederick John, ed. **The Achievement of D.H. Lawrence.** Norman, University of Oklahoma Press, 1953.

— — — — —. **Freudianism and the Literary Mind.** Baton Rouge, Louisiana State University Press, 1945.

Holtby, Winifred. **Virginia Woolf.** London, Wishart, 1932.

Hopkins, Annette Brown. **Elizabeth Gaskell.** London, J. Lehmann, 1952.

Hough, Graham. **The Dark Sun; a Study of D.H. Lawrence.** London, G. Duckworth, 1956.

House, Humphrey. **All in Due Time.** London, Rupert Hart-Davis, 1955.

Howarth, Robert Guy. **Literary Particles.** Sydney, Angus and Robertson, 1946.

Humphrey, Robert. **Stream of Consciousness in the Modern Novel.** University of California Press, 1954. (Perspectives in Criticism).

Hutchins, Patricia. **James Joyce's World.** London, Methuen, 1957.

Hutton, Richard Holt. **Essays on Some of the Modern Guides of English Thought in Matters of Faith.** London, Macmillan, 1914.

Jenkins, Elizabeth. **Henry Fielding.** London, Home & Van Thal, 1947.

Johnson, Edgar. **Charles Dickens, His Tragedy and Triumph.** New York, Simon and Schuster, 1952.

Johnstone, John Keith. **The Bloomsbury Group; a Study of E.M. Forster, Lytton Strachey, Virginia Woolf, and Their Circle.** London, Secker & Warburg, 1954.

Jones, William Powell. **James Joyce and the Common Reader.** Norman, University of Oklahoma Press, 1955.

Kahrl, George Morrow. **Tobias Smollett, Traveler-Novelist.** Chicago, University of Chicago Press, 1945.

Kain, Richard Morgan. **Fabulous Voyager.** Chicago, University of Chicago, 1947.

Kelman, John. **The Road; a Study of John Bunyan's "Pilgrim's Progress".** Edinburgh, Oliphant Anderson and Ferrier, 1912.

Twentieth Century Criticisms

Kenner, Hugh. **Wyndham Lewis.** London, Methuen, 1954.

Kettle, Arnold. **An Introduction to the English Novel.** London, Hutchinson's, 1951-53.

Kronenberger, Louis. **The Republic of Letters; Essays on Various Writers.** New York, Knopf, 1955.

Krutch, Joseph Wood. **Five Masters; a Study in the Mutations of the Novel.** New York, Cape & Smith, 1930.

Lafourcade, Georges. **Arnold Bennett.** London, Muller, 1939.

Laird, John. **Philosophical Incrusions Into English Literature.** Cambridge, England, University Press, 1946.

Leavis, F.R. **D.H. Lawrence, Novelist.** London, Chatto & Windus, 1955.

— — — — —. **The Great Tradition: George Eliot, Henry James, Joseph Conrad.** London, Chatto, 1948.

Leslie, Shane. **The Skull of Swift, an Extempore Exhumation.** Indianapolis, Bobbs-Merrill, 1928.

Levin, Harry. **James Joyce, a Critical Introduction.** Norfolk, New Directions, 1941.

Lewis, Wyndham. **Time and Western Man.** New York, Harcourt, 1928.

Lindsay, Jack. **George Meredith, His Life and Work.** London, Bodley Head, 1956.

— — — — —. **John Bunyan, Maker of Myths.** London, Methuen, 1937.

Linn, James Wever and Houghton Wells Taylor. **A Foreword to Fiction.** New York, Appleton-Century-Croft, 1935.

Loehrich, Rolf Rudolf. **The Secret of Ulysses.** McHenry, Ill., Compass Press, 1953.

Lowes, John Livingston. **Essays in Appreciation.** Boston, Houghton Mifflin, 1936.

— — — — —. **Of Reading Books; Four Essays.** London, Constable, 1930.

Lunn, Hugh Kingsmill. **Samuel Johnson.** by Hugh Kingsmill (pseud.) London, A. Barker, 1933.

Macaulay, Rose. **The Writings of E.M. Forster.** London, Hogarth Press, 1938.

MacCarthy, Sir Desmond. **Criticism.** London, Putnam, 1932.

McCullough, Bruce Welker. **Representative English Novelists: Defoe to Conrad.** New York, Harper, 1946.

Mackail, John William. **Studies in Humanism.** London, Longmans, Green, 1938.

McKechnie, James. **Meredith's Allegory, The Shaving of Shagpat.** London, Hodder and Stoughton, 1910.

McKillop, Alan Dugald. **The Early Masters of English Fiction.** Lawrence, University of Kansas Press, 1956.

Magalaner, Marven and Richard M. Karn. **Joyce, the Man, the Work, the Reputation.** New York, New York University Press, 1956.

Mais, Stuart P.B. **Why We Should Read.** New York, Dodd, Mead, 1921.

Matthews, James Brander. **The Historical Novel and Other Essays.** New York, Scribners, 1901.

Mauriac, Francois. **Great Men.** London, Rockcliff, 1952.

Twentieth Century Criticisms

Mehrotra, Kewal Krishna. **Horace Walpole and the English Novel; a Study of the Influence of "The Castle of Otranto", 1764-1820.** Oxford, B.Blackwell, 1934.

Mendilow, Adam Abraham. **Time and the Novel.** London, P. Nevill, 1952.

Mesnet, Marie Béatrice. **Graham Greene and the Heart of the Matter, an Essay.** London, Cresset Press, 1954.

Minnesota, University. **Forms of Modern Fiction.** Essays Collected in Honor of Joseph Warren Beach, ed. by William Van O'Connor. Minneapolis, University of Minnesota, 1948.

Monro, D.H. **Godwin's Moral Philosophy.** London, Oxford University Press, 1953.

Moore, Harry Thornton. **The Life and Works of D.H. Lawrence.** New York, Twayne Publishers, 1951.

Morf, Gustav. **The Polish Heritage of Joseph Conrad.** London, S. Low, Marston, 1930.

Mudrick, Marvin. **Jane Austen.** Princeton, Princeton University Press, 1952.

Muir, Edwin. **Transition; Essays in Contemporary Literature.** London, Leonard and Virginia Woolf, 1926.

Muller, Herbert Joseph. **Modern Fiction.** New York, Funk and Wagnals, 1937.

Murry, John Middleton. **Aspects of Literature.** New York, A.A. Knopf, 1920.

— — — — —. **D.H. Lawrence (Two Essays).** Cambridge, England, The Minority Press, 1930. (Minority Pamphlet No. 4).

— — — — —. **Jonathan Swift, a Critical Biography.** London, J. Cape, 1954.

Nejdefors-Frisk, Sonja. **George Moore's Naturalistic Prose.** Cambridge, Harvard University Press, 1952.

Nevinson, Henry Woodd. **Thomas Hardy.** London, G. Allen, 1941.

Newman, Bertram. **Jonathan Swift.** London, Allen & Unwin, 1937.

Newton, Deborah. **Virginia Woolf.** Melbourne University Press, 1946.

Noyes, Alfred. **The Opalescent Parrot.** London, Sheed & Ward, 1929.

Minnesota, University. **Forms of Modern Fiction; Essays Collected in Honor of Joseph Warren Beach,** ed. by William Van O'Connor. Minneapolis, University of Minnesota Press, 1948.

O'Donnell, Donat. **Maria Cross.** New York, Oxford University Press, 1952.

O'Faolain, Sean. **The Vanishing Hero: Studies in Novelists of the Twenties.** London, Eyre and Spottiswoode, 1956.

Pippett, Aileen. **The Moth and the Star: a Biography of Virginia Woolf.** Boston, Little, Brown, 1955.

Porter, Arthur. **The Inside of Bunyan's Dream.** London, The Religious Tract Society, 1927.

Potter, Stephen. **D.H. Lawrence; a First Study.** London, J. Cape, 1930.

Priestley, John Boynton. **The English Comic Characters.** London, J. Lane, 1928.

— — — — —. **Thomas Love Peacock.** New York, Macmillan, 1927. (English Men of Letters).

Pritchett, Victor Sawdon. **Books in General.** London, Chatto, 1953.

Twentieth Century Criticisms

Pritchett, Victor Sawdon. **The Living Novel.** New York, Reynal & Hitchcock, 1947.

Quennell, P.C. **The Singular Preference.** London, Collins, 1952.

Quintana, Ricardo. **The Mind and Art of Jonathan Swift.** London, Methuen, 1953.

— — — — —. **Swift: an Introduction.** London, Oxford University Press, 1955.

Rantavaara, Irma. **Virginia Woolf and Bloomsbury.** Helsinki, 1953.

Raphael, Alice Pearl. **Goethe, the Challenger.** New York, J. Cape and R. Ballou, 1932.

Ray, Gordon N. **Thackeray: the Age of Wisdom, 1847-1863.** New York, McGraw-Hill, 1958.

— — — — —. **Thackeray: the Uses of Adversity, 1811-1846.** New York, McGraw-Hill, 1955.

Rickword, Edgell. **Scrutinies.** Vol. II, London, Wishart, 1931.

Robertson, Leo. **Compton Mackenzie; an Appraisal of His Literary Work.** London, Richards Press, 1954.

Roditi, Edouard. **Oscar Wilde.** Norfolk, Conn., New Directions Books, 1947.

Rossi, Mario Manlio and Joseph M. Hone. **Swift; or The Egoist.** New York, Dutton, 1934.

S., C.P. **The Structure of "Wuthering Heights".** London, L. & Virginia Woolf, 1926. (Hogarth Essays. 19).

Sackville-West, Edward. **Inclinations.** London, Secker and Warburg, 1949.

Sadleir, Michael. **Things Past.** London, Constable, 1944.

Saintsbury, George Edward Bateman. **A Consideration of Thackeray.** London, Oxford University Press, 1931.

— — — — —. **A Saintsbury Miscellany.** New York, Oxford University Press, 1947.

Sanders, Gerald De Witt. **Elizabeth Gaskell.** New Haven, Yale University Press, 1929.

Savage, Derek S. **The Withered Branch; Six Studies in the Modern Novel.** London, Eyre & Spottiswoode, 1950.

Scott, Nathan A. **Rehearsals of Discomposure.** New York, King's Crown Press, 1952.

Schutte, William M. **Joyce and Shakespeare: a Study in the Meaning of "Ulysses".** New Haven, Yale University Press, 1957.

Scott-James, Rolfe Arnold. **Personality in Literature, 1913-1931.** New York, Holt, 1932.

Sen, C. **Daniel De Foe, His Mind and Art.** Calcutta, University of Calcutta, 1948.

Sharrock, Roger. **John Bunyan.** London, Hutchinson's University Library, 1954.

Shepperson, Archibald Bolling. **The Novel in Motley, a History of the Burlesque Novel in English.** Cambridge, Harvard University Press, 1936.

Simons, J.B. **Arnold Bennett and His Novels.** Oxford, B. Blackwell, 1936.

Smidt, Kristian. **James Joyce and the Cultic Use of Fiction.** Oslo, Okademisk Forlay, 1955.

Smith, Paul Jordan. **A Key to the "Ulysses" of James Joyce.** New York, Covici, 1934.

Twentieth Century Criticisms

Smith, Sophie Shilleto. **Dean Swift.** London, Methuen, 1910.

Spark, Muriel. **Child of Light, a Reassessment of Mary Wollstonecraft Shelley.** Hadleigh, Essex, Tower Bridge Publications, 1951.

— — — — — and Derek Stanford. **Emily Brontë, Her Life and Work.** London, Owen, 1953.

Speare, Morris Edmund. **The Political Novel.** New York, Oxford University Press, 1924.

Spender, Stephen. **The Creative Element.** London, H. Hamilton, 1953.

Spilka, Mark. **The Love Ethic of D.H. Lawrence.** Bloomington, Indiana University Press, 1955.

Stanford, W.B. **The Ulysses Theme; A Study in the Adaptability of a Traditional Hero.** Oxford, Basil Blackwell, 1954.

Stephen, Sir Leslie. **George Eliot.** London, Macmillan, 1902.

— — — — — — —. **Studies of a Biographer.** New York, Putnam's 1907.

Stevenson, Lionel. **The Ordeal of George Meredith, a Biography.** New York, Scribner, 1953.

Stewart, Douglas Alexander. **The Flesh and the Spirit, an Outlook on Literature.** Sydney, Angus and Robertson, 1948.

Stillman, Clara Gruening. **Samuel Butler, a Mid-Victorian Modern.** New York, Viking Press, 1932.

Stock, Irvin. **William Hale White (Mark Rutherford); a Critical Study.** London, Allen and Unwin, 1956.

Stoll, Elmer Edgar. **From Shakespeare to Joyce.** Garden City, New York, Doubleday, Doran, 1944.

Strong, Leonard Alfred George. **Personal Remarks.** London, P. Nevill, 1953.

— — — — —. **The Sacred River; an Approach to James Joyce.** London, Methuen, 1949.

Swinnerton, Frank Arthur. **George Gissing, a Critical Study.** London, Secker, 1912.

Talon, Henri Antoine. **John Bunyan, the Man and His Works.** London, Rockliff, 1951.

Taylor, William Duncan. **Jonathan Swift, a Critical Essay.** London, Davies, 1933.

Thompson, Harold William. **A Scottish Man of Feeling.** London, Oxford University Press, 1931.

Thompson, Lawrence. **A Comic Principle in Sterne-Meredith-Joyce.** Oslo, British Institute, 1954.

Thomson, Clara Linklater. **Samuel Richardson; a Biographical and Critical Study.** London, H. Marshall, 1900.

Thornbury, Ethel Margaret. **Henry Fielding's Theory of the Comic Prose Epic.** Madison, University of Wisconsin, 1931.

Tillotson, Geoffrey. **Criticism and the Nineteenth Century.** London, Athlone Press, 1951.

Tillotson, Kathleen Mary. **Novels of the Eighteen-Forties.** Oxford, Clarendon Press, 1954.

Tillyard, Eustace Mandeville Wetenhall. **The English Epic and Its Background.** New York, Oxford University Press, 1954.

Tindall, William York. **James Joyce; His Way of Interpreting the Modern World.** New York, Scribner, 1950.

— — — — —. **The Literary Symbol.** New York, Columbia University Press, 1955.

Twentieth Century Criticisms

Traugott, John Lewis. **Tristram Shandy's World.** Berkeley, University of California Press, 1954.

Trilling, Lionel. **E.M. Forster.** Norfolk, Conn., New Directions, 1943.

— — — — —. **The Opposing Self; Nine Essays in Criticism.** New York, Viking Press, 1955.

Turner, Albert Morton. **The Making of "The Cloister and the Hearth."** Chicago, University of Chicago Press, 1938.

Van Doren, Mark. **The Private Reader.** New York, Holt, 1942.

Van Ghent, Dorothy. **The English Novel.** New York, Rinehart, 1953.

Varma, Devendra P. **The Gothic Flame.** London, Arthur Barker, 1957.

Verschoyle, Derek, ed. **The English Novelists; a Survey of the Novel by Twenty Contemporary Novelists.** London, Chatto, 1936.

Wagner, Geoffrey Atheling. **Wyndham Lewis; A Portrait of the Artist as Enemy.** London, Routledge and K. Paul, 1957.

Waldock, Arthur John Alfred. **James Joyce and Others.** London, Williams & Norgate, 1937.

Watson, Francis. **Daniel Defoe.** London, Longmans, Green, 1952.

Watt, Ian. **The Rise of the Novel; Studies in Defoe, Richardson and Fielding.** London, Chatto and Windus, 1957.

Webster, Harvey Curtis. **On a Darkling Plain.** Chicago, University of Chicago Press, 1947.

West, Ray Benedict. ed., **Essays in Modern Literary Criticism.** New York, Rinehart, 1952.

West, Rebecca. **The Strange Necessity; Essays.** Garden City,

Doubleday, 1928.

Whalley, George. **Poetic Process.** London, Routledge and Kegan Paul, 1953.

Wharey, James Blanton. **A Study of the Sources of Bunyan's Allegories.** Baltimore, J.H. Furst, 1904.

Whibley, Charles. **William Makepeace Thackeray.** New York, Dodd, 1903.

Whipple, Edwin Percy. **Charles Dickens; the Man and His Work.** Boston, Houghton Mifflin, 1912.

Wickham, Harvey. **The Impuritans.** New York, Dial Press, 1929.

Wiley, Paul L. **Conrad's Measure of Man.** Madison, University of Wisconsin Press, 1954.

Willcock, Mary Patricia. **Bunyan Calling; a Voice from the Seventeenth Century.** London, Allen & Unwin, 1944.

Williams, Randall. **The Wessex Novels of Thomas Hardy.** London, Dent, 1924.

Williams, Raymond. **Reading and Criticism.** London, F. Muller, 1950.

Willis, Irene Cooper. **The Authorship of "Wuthering Heights."** London, Hogarth Press, 1936.

Wilson, Edmund. **Axel's Castle; a Study in the Imaginative Literature of 1870-1930.** New York, Scribner, 1939.

— — — — —. **Classics and Commercials.** New York, Farrar, Straus, 1950.

— — — — —. **The Shores of Light.** New York, Farrar, Straus and Young, 1952.

— — — — —. **The Triple Thinkers.** London, J. Lehmann, 1952.

Twentieth Century Criticisms

Wilson, Edmund. **The Wound and the Bow.** New York, Oxford University Press, 1947.

Woodcock, George. **William Godwin.** London, Porcupine Press, 1946.

Woolf, Virginia (Stephen). **The Common Reader.** Second Series. London, L. and Virginia Woolf at the Hogarth Press, 1932.

— — — — —. **The Moment and Other Essays.** London, Hogarth, 1947.

Wright, Andrew H. **Jane Austen's Novels.** London, Chatto, 1953.

Wright, Clifford Kent. **Bunyan as a man of Letters.** Oxford, B.H. Blackwell, 1916.

Wright, Thomas. **The Life of Daniel Defoe.** Bi-Centenary ed. London, C.J. Farncombe, 1931.

Wright, Walter Francis. **Art and Substance in George Meredith, a Study in Narrative.** Lincoln, University of Nebraska Press, 1953.

— — — — —. **Romance and Tragedy in Joseph Conrad.** Lincoln, University of Nebraska Press, 1949.

Zabel, Morton Dauwen. **Craft and Character in Modern Fiction.** New York, Viking, 1957.

— — — — —. **Literary Opinion in America; Essays Illustrating the Status, Methods and Problems of Criticism in the Twentieth Century.** New York, Harper, 1951.

Zandvoort, R.W. **Sidney's Arcadia.** Amsterdam, Swets & Zeitlinger, 1929.

PERIODICALS

Accent

American Review

American Scholar

Atlantic Monthly

Blackwood's

Brontë Society. Publications.

Cambridge Journal

College English

Columbia University Studies in English and Comparative Literature

Critique: Studies in Modern Fiction

Dalhousie Review

Dial

ELH (English Literary History)

English

Englische Review

English Association. Essays and Studies.

English Association. Leaflet.

English Association Pamphlet

The English Journal

English Studies

Essays in Criticism

Harvard Studies in English

Horizon

Hudson Review

Twentieth Century Criticisms

James Joyce Yearbook

Journal of English and Germanic Philology

Journal of General Education

Kenyon Review

Modern Fiction Studies

Modern Language Notes

Modern Language Quarterly

Modern Language Review

Modern Philology

New Mexico Quarterly

Nineteenth Century Fiction

North American Review

Northwestern University Studies. Humanities Series.

Orion

Pacific Spectator

Partisan Review

Philological Quarterly

PMLA (Publications of the Modern Language Association)

Proceedings of the British Academy

Queen's Quarterly

Review of English Studies

Scrutiny

Sewanee Review

Shenandoah

South Atlantic Quarterly

Southerly

Southern Review

Studies in Philology

Transactions of the Royal Society of Literature

Twentieth Century

Twentieth Century Literature

University of California. Publications. English Studies.

University of California Publications in English

University of Illinois Studies in Language and Literature

University of Kansas City Review

University of Michigan Contributions in Modern Philology

University of Texas Studies in English

University of Toronto Quarterly

Virginia Quarterly Review

Western Humanities Review

Western Review

Yale Review

Twentieth Century Criticisms

WITHDRAWN from the Alma College Library